How To Write Your Personal & Family History

A Resource Manual

By Keith E. Banks

Published 1988 By

HERITAGE BOOKS, INC.
1540E Pointer Ridge Place, Bowie, Maryland 20716
(301)-390-7709

ISBN 1-55613-143-7

A Complete Catalog Listings Hundreds Of Titles On
History, Genealogy, And Americana
Available Free Upon Request

To the unborn children of the world. It is they who must carry the torch when we have run our race, no matter how far or how well we ran.

"It is good to look to the past to gain appreciation for the present and perspective for the future. It is good to look upon the virtues of those who have gone before, to gain strength for whatever lies ahead. It is good to reflect upon the work of those who labored so hard and gained so little in this world, but out of whose dreams and early plans, so well nurtured, has come a great harvest of which we are the beneficiaries. Their tremendous example can become a compelling motivation for us all, for each of us is a pioneer in his own life."

Gordon B. Hinckley, *Ensign*, July 1984. Copyright 1984 by The Church of Jesus Christ of Latter-day Saints. Used by permission.

TABLE OF CONTENTS

Appendices

ACKNOWLEDGMENTS

Family history is a family affair. Likewise, so has the creation of this book been a family affair. I may have written the words, but much of the credit should go to my parents, by brother, my wife, and my children. It is they who instilled in me a desire to preserve the story of my family, and a desire to share some of what I have learned with others.

More specifically, I want to thank my wife, Joycelyn, for her ever-constant love, encouragement, and support. She read and re-read every sentence I composed, and offered valuable advice and suggestions on ways I could improve what I was trying to say. She never complained about my many hours at the library, making copies, or at the computer. She is a great editor, and my best friend.

I want to also thank Nathan and Ryan, my two oldest sons, for allowing me to publish stories about experiences they find embarrassing. I tried to be fair by including experiences that embarrass me (and Joycelyn), also.

My brother, Roger, and my mom and dad deserve credit for their research into the local history of Huntsville, Alabama. Their efforts helped me both in the writing of this book and in the writing of our own family history.

I greatly appreciate the time that Jim Parrish took out of his busy schedule to create the many illustrations found throughout this book and on the cover. His visual imagery enhanced and complemented the written text in ways I could have never done myself.

Hopefully the book we have all created will be of benefit to many other ordinary folks wishing to leave something of value behind when they've departed this life for bigger and better things.

K.E.B.

INTRODUCTION

Personal History. What is it? Simply stated, it is a record of a person's life. Family history is merely an extension to include the other human beings who share that earthly sojourn with us. It can take many forms, from a simple photo album to a short history to a fully researched and documented biography. It may also be the traditions we pass down from one generation to another, or a collection of old love letters gathering dust in a hidden box in the attic. Whatever form it takes, it is an historical record that has the potential of surviving the ravages of time, bearing silent witness of our existence, and of our joys and sorrows to a future world.

Experts estimate that in the history of our earth there have been approximately one hundred billion people who have lived and died. Each and every one of these lives has been unique and significantly different from any other; no two persons' life experiences have been the same. Yet out of those billions of people, we know very little about the individual lives of more than a few thousand people. Of the five billion human beings alive today, only a handful will be remembered a mere century from now.

This book is a resource manual to aid you in preserving your own personal and family histories. In it you'll find scores of ideas on how to compile, write, record, and pass on the record of your life to future generations. This is not just another book on how to write your autobiography, though you will find a chapter devoted to the subject. In addition, you'll find chapters devoted to creative ways of keeping a journal or diary; setting up family archives; writing a chronology; creating pictorial histories; preserving important family documents; conducting and transcribing oral histories; beginning genealogy research; writing special studies; reproduction and binding; and much, much more.

Using this book, you'll be able to begin or expand your personal and family histories. Whether you're a grandfather, housewife, writer, genealogist (not to be confused with gynecologist!), or student, you'll find ideas you can apply to your own research and writing. The words you write today will be cherished by your descendants for generations to come, and might even be quoted by historians centuries from now as they try to explain life in the twentieth century.

This manual is divided into three parts. Part I, **In The Beginning** . . ., should be read first. It will motivate and encourage you, and give you an overview of each of the history projects in this book. You will also learn how to conduct research into your own and family's past, and the basics of writing family history. The rest of this book may be read (or preferably, *used*) in any sequence, and should be adapted to help you in the creation of your own, unique and individual, family history library. Some history projects are quite simple, taking only a few days or weeks to complete. Others, like the autobiography, could take many months to complete.

There are few skills prerequisite to the creation of a family history. There are no rules that must be observed, nor is there any one "accepted" way of doing it. One doesn't need years of education to become a family historian. The day you sit down and begin to compile your first chronology (or any other historical document or study) is the day you become a family historian. The documents you create will be of as great a worth (probably greater) to future generations as the volumes of stuffy dissertations and boring textbooks produced by PhDs each year. For *you* this book was written.

PART I
IN THE BEGINNING...

CHAPTER 1
The Psychology Of Family History

Why should we learn about history? Millions of students ask themselves, their parents, and their teachers this question every year. It's not always an easy question to answer. After all, knowing what year the Magna Charta was signed (and by whom) isn't a prerequisite to any jobs I've ever heard of, other than history teachers.

History is important, however. In fact, a knowledge of history is essential. This chapter is my attempt to not only convince you of this great and eternal truth (kind of like E=MC2), but to also get you *excited* about learning, and especially writing (or preserving) personal and family history.

History - What is it?

For the purposes of this book, history is two things. First, it is a record of man's past. Second, and most important, it is the actual events of the past themselves. God may have created the world, the heavens, the oceans, the animals, and even man, but man created his own history. Every person who has ever lived has made some contribution to the history of the world. They've made an even greater contribution to the history of their own family.

In fact, history literally flows from us all. As we proceed from one microsecond to the next, our actions *become* history. One might even argue that the only lasting contibution any man or woman makes in this world, is in the creation of history.   Whether an action is good or bad, large or small, it is something that cannot be changed. Once an action is done, it slips quickly and quietly into the irretrievabe realm of the past.

3

I also said that history was a *record* of man's past. This, however, is a secondary definition. After all, such a record is not essential. And no matter how hard we try to preserve what has happened to man over the course of history, we can never hope to completely recreate the conditions that led up to certain decisions and actions. It is this aspect of history, however, with which this book concerns itself. We create history just by the very act of living; preserving and writing that history requires a conscious effort.

Where Did You Come From?

The Irish novelist Kathleen Coyle said, "It is absurd to think that life begins for us at birth. The pattern is set far back; we merely step into the process." Virtually everyone with any understanding at all will agree that much of what we are is a product of our parents and our environment. But it didn't begin with them. There is a reason they raised us and disciplined us the way they did; a cause which may go back many generations. Were your parents frugal with money because of their experiences during the Great Depression, or was it a result of shortages experienced by *their* grandparents during the Civil War?

A complete knowledge of self requires more than just a memory of past actions. It also requires a knowledge of why you believe the way you do, and why you made the decisions you have made. One readily recognizes the many differences between cultures, but the differences between families *within* a culture can be just as significant. Without a knowledge of your family's past, you can never hope to completely understand yourself. Your physical tie to previous generations may have been cut at birth, but your psychological ties to the past are eternal.

Writing History: The Past

There are many different reasons for writing personal history. I will discuss three: understanding our ancestors and their influence upon us; remembering our own lives and understanding ourselves; and teaching our children.

I've already discussed how learning of our family's past will lead to a greater understanding of ourselves. But there is also another reward, one that is difficult to understand without actually experiencing it. As we begin to learn about our ancestors and the lives they lived, we begin to identify with them, and appreciate the contribution they made to us. It's

4

almost like being reunited with a long-lost friend; a person who has been a tremendous influence in our life.

As a son or daughter, it is difficult to see our parents and grandparents as individuals, much like ourselves, who were also once young children and had to grow and learn the same things we've gone through. But unless we can let down our defenses as children and see them as people much like our friends and ourselves, our understanding of them will always be distorted and our relationships strained.

It is a sad and mistaken notion in our society today that the role of parenting ends after a mere 18 or 20 years. Parents are always ahead of their children in gaining experience and wisdom. The parent who stops parenting misses out on being a continuing and important influence to their posterity. The result is often loneliness and depression. The son or daughter who cuts off their parents is destined to only learn of life through experience, whether good or bad. The experiences of countless generations before are ignored, and little progress is made from one generation to the next.

As you begin to talk to your parents, grandparents, aunts, and uncles, about their lives, you'll be surprised to find out how human they are. As you express interest in learning about them, and their lives, you'll find you've discovered a friend, not just a relative.

This is especially true with the elderly. They are perhaps our greatest resource as a society, and are also the most neglected. There is so much that we could learn from them, if we would only listen. What lessons have they learned from their long lives? If they could do it over again, what would they do differently, and why? What did they think was important when they were young adults, and how have their views changed over the years? Why? Now that they've lived a full life, what do they think is most important? What advice would they leave for their descendents?

From a knowledge of their lives and experiences, we can better prepare for our own future. Are we so naive to believe that their lives are not relevent to ours, that our experiences will be so different from their own? When we are young we often think like this, but as we mature and gain our own experience we usually find that, even though the world around us may change dramatically, the life-processes of man remain virtually unchanged.

Don't make the mistake of thinking that because an ancestor "didn't amount to anything" there is nothing to be learned from his or her life. There are lessons to be learned from everyone who has ever lived. The things we might learn from a man who spent his life in and out of prison are just as important as the things we might learn from a president or millionaire. At some point in their lives they were possibly on the same road, headed in the same direction. Each made a change, seemingly small at the time, in their direction which eventually led to where they are today.

Writing about our family's past helps us appreciate the present, the time in which we are living our own lives. No matter how bad things may seem in our own life at the time, we need only look to the past to find harder times. Our ancestors survived; so will we. The sun will rise again tomorrow, the same as it has for eons past. Some things never change.

Writing History: The Present

So far we've mostly discussed preserving the lives of past generations, both for their benefit and ours. Most of this book, however, is devoted to preserving our own lives, writing about the present.

As I mentioned before, we create history just by the act of living. We spend twenty-four hours a day making history, yet we do little to remember the things which we've done. How many people can remember what they did on May 22, 1985? Yet at the time, that was the most important day in their life; it was *the present.* Can you remember what *you* did that day? Do you remember *anything* of significance that you did during the entire month of May that year? How about May, 1975? May, 1965?

What do you remember about your first day of high school? How did you feel? What did you wear? What were your hopes and dreams for the future? Who was the first boy or girl you kissed? What did you feel? Were you scared?

Some people have better recall than others. Often, even when we do remember some things, certain facts become distorted with time or become confused with other memories. What did you get for Christmas when you were 12 years old? Are you sure it was *that* Christmas, or could it have been the one before or after? Are you sure it wasn't a birthday present?

Perhaps the greatest benefit to keeping a journal or diary or any other type of personal history is the power it has to enlarge our memory. Even just a short sentence about some happening, written in a diary many years ago, will often trigger a complete recall of the event in our conscious mind.

Recording details about our present lives is often difficult, as we almost always feel that we'll remember the things that are now important to us. How could we ever forget our best friend's name? Ridiculous! It isn't possible that we could forget all those cute little words our one-year-old is saying, is it?

Of course, we should know by now, we *will* forget. And as we get older, we will forget even more. Ironically, later years is usually the time we most want to remember our younger days. Our busy lives are slowing down, and we find joy in reliving and reflecting upon our past.

We should record the trivial as well as life-changing events. We should include conversations, illnesses, observations, and all other kinds of things that make up our daily lives. If we're trying to resolve a problem, we should include details of our efforts; not only our successes, but also our failures.

Writing about difficult times in our lives can actually help us to cope with them. You can express emotions in your private writing that might be detrimental if released in other ways, and oftentimes you will view events with a different perspective with the passage of time.

Writing about ourselves also helps us to see ourselves more objectively. We seldom take the time to analyze our own actions and behavior. Once we do something, we usually put it behind us and move on. Going back and writing about our lives, however, forces us to review our motives and reactions to others, and to consciously prepare for similar situations in the future.

There are many ways of preserving your own life other than keeping a journal or writing an autobiography. Well-organized photo albums provide a valuable record of your life. So do collections of old letters. In the chapters that follow you will find dozens of other ways in which you can preserve your personal and family history. Whatever form it takes, there needs to be a conscious effort in the compiling of family history to preserve memories. Unorganized, they are easily neglected, difficult to use, and possibly even discarded.

Writing History: The Future

It is my own opinion that the greatest reason for preserving family history is for *the future*. Our children, and our children's children. After all, there is nothing we can do to change the past. There are some things we can do as individuals to influence life in the present, but our greatest potential for affecting what will some day also be history, is the possible influence we have upon our descendents.

If that sounds confusing, look at it this way. You are but one individual. More than likely, you have no great amount of power over or influence upon our world today. But if you have two children, and each of them has two or three children, and so on and so forth, within a mere century from now there could be more than 50 individuals descended directly from you. In two hundred years, that number could be more than 1000! If you leave no record of yourself, your life *will* be forgotten. An article in the Salt Lake City *Deseret News* more than one hundred years ago said:

"If a man keeps no diary, the path crumbles away behind him as his feet leave it; and days gone by are but little more than a blank, broken by a few distorted shadows. His life is all confined within the limits of today . . . . There must be a richness about the life of a person who keeps a diary . . . . And a million more little links and ties must bind him to the members of his family circle, and to all among whom he lives." (July 16, 1862)

If you diligently record your comings and goings, your failures and successes, your feelings about the world, about life, etc., many of your descendents will be influenced, to some degree, by your writings. And each of these people will have some influence upon the world around them.

Even if you have had little influence in your own lifetime upon those around you, a personal history or journal may make you a great teacher and leader to your posterity. The written word takes on a life of its own, and is often accepted, right or wrong, as truth. It can be read at leisure; it can be studied; and it can be absorbed into our own life experience. Words that may sound preachy when uttered by a parent to an adolescent child may become great words of wisdom when put in black and white and read at a later time. The words may direct and edify persons unknown at a time long removed from whence they were first recorded; they may bring comfort during times of sorrow, and solutions in times of crisis.

A man or woman can bequeath no greater gift to their posterity than a full account of their life and what they learned from it. It is a gift that can be given no matter how simple a life one may have led, or how poor in worldly goods they may have been.

It seems odd that people will sacrifice and spend thousands of dollars to buy tombstones on which they record the names of their parents, and the dates that mark the beginning and end of their lives. For a great deal less money, and

8

with only a little more time and effort, they could create a written or recorded memorial that would preserve a memory of that person's life. The gravestone will be of little or no value in only a few generations, however a personal history increases in value with each passing generation.

For Additional Help . . .

There are many sources of help and inspiration for preparing your family history. If you need help writing, join a writer's club. Check out books at your local library on writing. I've tried to include many ideas and ways for recording your history in this book, however the possibilities are limited only by your imagination.

Many articles appearing in magazines each year are devoted to keeping journals, writing autobiographies, researching genealogy, and the like. Some colleges even offer courses on these subjects. The Church of Jesus Christ of Latter Saints, which operates the largest genealogical library in the world, actively encourages its members to prepare personal and family histories.

If you need further encouragement, read other books and magazine articles on the subject. What I've included in this book is what I've learned from others, and my own experience writing my own family's history. As you progress in writing your own personal and family history, you will undoubtedly incorporate what you learned from this book, other people's writings, and your own experience. Whatever method(s) you decide to use, resolve now to begin recording your life, and then *do it*!

CHAPTER 2
First Things First

Before undertaking any great adventure, it is always best to plan. To chart a course, so to speak. This is especially true when starting a personal or family history. Many individuals excited about writing their history have been quickly overwhelmed by the perceived enormity of the project, and have given up before they really got started.

In this resource manual, family history refers to more than just a book - it is a *library*. This chapter briefly discusses each of the family history projects covered in this book, and offers suggestions on how you might chart your course as you begin this great work.

It would be nice if there was an easy step-by-step method to writing your family history, but there isn't. I could tell you what worked for me, but that might not be what will work best for you. What I do suggest is this: read through the project descriptions that follow, and then pick one that will be fairly easy (and won't take too long) for you to accomplish. Once you've completed a couple of the easier projects, you'll be more confident of your abilities as a family historian, and you'll be ready to tackle any of the more difficult ones.

Journals, Diaries

If you don't ever do anything else, begin now to keep a personal journal. It doesn't have to be written in every day; many people write only once a week. It doesn't need to be an all-encompassing record of your everyday life either. You may choose to write only about one aspect of your life, such as your job, a hobby, or perhaps just your social life or children. However you decide to do it, start your journal this week, and make it a life-long habit. Of all the history projects in this book, this one is the easiest to start, but it requires dedication to stick with it week after week, year after year.

Photos, Movies

Just about everyone nowadays owns a camera and has taken hundreds (if not thousands) of pictures of family, friends, and vacations. Perhaps without realizing it, millions of people are already involved in creating a family history as they organize priceless photographs into albums, videotape birthday parties, and put together slide shows of their most recent family vacation.

There are other aspects of life as worthy of being documented on film, however, as the highlights and turning points that most people are already photographing. These include pictures and movies of our everyday lives. After all, most of our time is occupied by repetitious (yet easily forgotten) acts, our jobs, and mundane chores. How many people take photographs of Mom cooking dinner, Dad at work, Sister putting on make-up (but be careful - this could get you in touble), or Brother cutting the grass?

Additionally, photographs need to be properly identified and cared for. There are millions of pictures in attics and basements that nobody remembers who the people in them are. The same thing will happen to your own pictures if you don't somehow mark them. They will be of little value to your descendents if they don't know why the pictures were important to you, why you took them, and why you kept them.

Pictures may also be used to illustrate virtually every other project covered in this manual. These pictorial histories, chronologies, and special studies add immeasurably to the value and interest of your family library. Photographs are easily added at any point of research and writing, all the way up to the time of final preparation for printing and reproduction.

Baby, Graduation, & Wedding Books

Just about everyone who has a baby buys (or receives) a baby book to record the infant's early years of growth and development. There are similar books published for weddings and graduation. It is also possible to create your own "custom made" book, which may be used to document a big vacation, or perhaps a family reunion. The trick is filling in the blanks once you have these books. They are a valuable part of your family history library, and should be used to document many of the big events in your life.

Letters

Don't throw those old letters away! Next to a personal journal, letters can give us more detail concerning our everyday lives than just about any other source. A collection of old love letters can make an exciting book in and of itself. Quotes from old letters are especially good for illustrating other works, such as a biography. Just organize and hang on to them for now, and you'll find uses for them later.

Another type of letter that is becoming increasingly popular is the family newsletter. Many families send them out at Christmas. They range from simple one-page handwritten and copied letters to elaborate, type-set, professional quality newsletters. Keep those that you receive, and consider starting one yourself. It's an easy way to stay in touch with many friends and relatives, and despite what some writers to Dear Abby have said, most people enjoy receiving them. A collection of these newsletters you've sent out over the years will become a valuable part of your family archives.

Documents

Your family documents are your most valuable records. They're the "proof" that what you say in your writing elsewhere is true. Your birth certificate "proves" that you were born at a given place on a certain day. Likewise, the speeding ticket you got in New York last year while on vacation "proves" that you were there when you said you were (it also "proves" a few other things!).

Your documents need to be organized, and properly cared for to ensure their long life. Gather them together in one place - cardboard boxes will do as a start - and then decide how you want to keep them permanently. Doing this in the beginning is fairly easy, and will help you when conducting research for other projects.

You don't want these important documents to be lost or damaged, and there are many times you need to view them for reference (especially when compiling your family history). Why not make copies of all of them, and bind the copies together in a book along with a document list? They will always be together in one place when you need to find them, and the book can be put on the shelf with your other family history publications. This is a fairly easy project, once you've gathered all of your documents.

Chronology

An extensive chronology of your life is an essential ingredient of your family history. It is also one of the easiest projects to compile and update, and it should be one of your first priorities. You will find it to be a great tool in the creation of your other family history projects. Don't worry about not being able to remember the exact dates when things happened; approximations are good enough for your first draft. You'll find many of these dates later as you do further research and conduct oral histories.

The timetable is similar to the chronology, with an added dimension. The major events in your own life are listed along with major world events, which puts your life in its true context within the era in which you live. With the aid of popular **Timetables** books (can be found in most libraries), it's an easy project to complete, after you've compiled your chronology. A timeline is similar, creating a graphic display of your life and world events together on one chart.

A Short History

A short individual or family history is one of the easier projects covered in this book. They may be as short as one page (similar to a resume), or as long as twenty or thirty pages. They can often be written completely from your own personal knowledge or memory. Such a history can help you determine what areas of your life you want to cover in more detail in other projects, which aspects of your life warrant special treatment (such as a special study), and where you want to proceed next.

Special Studies

There are an endless number of special studies that can be conducted in family history. They may be very short and simple, like the short history, or they can be more involved than an extensive biography. You may want to write about your activity in high school sports, or about your involvement with a favorite hobby. A good topic to cover would be your work history, covering such aspects as parental influences, education, part-time jobs, career changes, etc. Another special study might just cover boyfriends, girlfriends, or other close relationships.

Lists, Maps

An important ingredient of many projects are lists. Examples include: places lived, schools attended, teachers, jobs, family income (by year), favorite books or movies, cars owned, - the list goes on and on. Some lists will be of special value to other projects, and you'll want to include them as appendices.

Maps can be used to identify important places in your family's history. Places that seem familiar to you and your family may be unknown to your descendents living hundreds or thousands of miles (or years) away. Place names and boundaries may even change over the years. You can also use maps to illustrate big trips and family vacations.

Annual History

An annual history is a summary of last year's activities. Written while the memories are still fresh, it will provide a wealth of information to your children and your children's children. When beginning your family history, it's much easier trying to reconstruct just your last year than it is to remember and cover everything in your whole life up to the present. Beginning to write annual histories now will make your job as a family historian much easier in the future. This is another project you can begin immediately.

Biography: Individual & Family

A biography or autobiography, whether individual or of a family, is an ambitious project to undertake. After all, it is the story of an entire life or lives. Unless you have a lot of time to devote to it, a biography may take you a long time to complete. It's a rewarding project however, and should definitely be included in your library. The actual writing and organization isn't difficult - it just takes time.

Oral History

An oral history is a tape recorded interview with someone, or perhaps even just one person narrating their life story into a tape recorder. Oral histories are valuable in that they preserve a person's voice and speech mannerisms for future

15

generations, long after that person has passed away. When transcribed, they are enjoyable and easy to read. An oral history interview can be completed in as little as half an hour, and a transcript prepared in only a few days. Never pass up the opportunity to conduct an oral history with your family members, especially those who are elderly. Not only will they add immeasurably to your family history library, but they will also bring you and your family closer together as you express interest in their lives.

Genealogy

A genealogy is an essential ingredient of your family history. It shows who your parents were and who their parents were, and is what links you to everyone else who has ever lived on this planet. Take the time, early in your family history research, to fill out a pedigree chart and family group sheets for your family's genealogy. Genealogical research is extremely easy to begin, and may lead to a life-long hobby in and of itself.

Who's Who in Family History

Everyone has seen a **Who's Who** type of book. Normally they list the outstanding individuals in a given geographical area or career field. In a family history who's who, however, you list all of your family members, friends (enemies too, if you like), and co-workers, with a sentence or two or paragraph about each of them and your relationship with them. This can be an easy on-going project while you work on other things; it may take time to remember the names of people from earlier periods of your life.

Other Projects

There are many other projects you'll want to include as part of your family history. Some I've included in this book are: creating a family coat of arms; designing and making a family flag; carving a family history totem pole, compiling a cookbook of your family's favorite recipes; making a "family history" quilt; writing short stories from your family's history for publication in newspapers and magazines; collecting and displaying artifacts from your family's history; compiling a family health history; and when you've completed everything listed in this book and run out of ideas of your own, creating a comprehensive index of all your work.

Reproduction & Binding Methods

Once you've finished writing your first family history project, you'll want to put it in a finished and bound form to place on your bookshelf. There are several ways your "camera-ready" pages can be reproduced. The simplest, and the least expensive is to photocopy them yourself at one of the many "quick-print" shops around town. If you want better quality, or many copies, you'll probably want to go with off-set printing.

There are many ways that your family histories can be bound. A three-ring binder works well for your draft copies as you're writing, however you'll want something more permanent for your final copy. Having an embossed hardcover is the most expensive, but it will last nearly forever and should be considered for your most important projects. The easiest and least expensive are the plastic binders which many printers can bind your documents with for only a few dollars.

Tradition

Every family has traditions, with those centered around the holidays being the most dear and remembered. Traditions are one of mankind's oldest forms of family history; the ones you start with your own family may very well be passed down from one generation to the next.

Children & Family History

You should try early on to interest your children in your family's history. There are many ways to get them started keeping a journal, and there are a multitude of family activities that will not only teach your children about your family's heritage, but will also bring your own family closer together in the process. It is your children and your children's children that you're creating this history for; help them to see the contribution and lasting good they can accomplish, even while they're young.

CHAPTER 3
Research

Many people shake and tremble when they hear the word *RESEARCH*. They envision cavernous libraries with dusty old books and little old ladies who ride brooms to work. Or nowadays, they fear being silently laughed at by a sophisticated computer terminal every time they make an error trying to access information.

Research, however, can actually be fun. It's just a matter of perspective. To enjoy research, one must think of it as a puzzle, like a mystery to be solved. Each clue leads to a new source. As our investigation continues, we get closer and closer to solving the case. Eventually, after much work following false leads and dead ends, we finally discover the facts we were looking for. Case closed.

Research is seldom easy, but one always learns from conducting research. Even if you never find the particular fact you are looking for, you will find other pertinent information and bits of trivia along the way. Actually, the longer it takes for you to find something, the more you will learn from the experience. But it can be frustrating sometimes.

Sources

In historical research, sources are usually divided into two general categories. Primary sources are those written or communicated by people experiencing an event firsthand. Secondary sources are those which are compiled from primary sources. For example, when a newspaper reporter interviews an eye-witness, he is using a primary source to write his story. When finished, however, the article becomes a secondary source to future researchers; it was written by someone who got the story from someone else. It is always best to use primary sources when conducting historical research.

19

Where to Go?

All resources (places to look for primary and secondary sources) for conducting research fall into three general categories. Our first resource is **ourselves**. What do we know or remember about the subject? The second resource is **o t h e r s** . Who can we contact that has knowledge of what we are looking for? Lastly, is what I call **library**. This includes all written or recorded information, whether located in libraries or elsewhere. We will discuss each of these resources in the order in which they are best used.

Ourselves

The easiest information to access is what we have locked within our own memory. Even if we don't know the exact date when something happened in the past, we can usually make a close estimate. We know better than anyone else what we did, and why we did it. Even if we learned a story second-hand from a parent or grandparent, we can record what we remember of the event, and then seek other sources to verify and embellish what we have recorded.

Others

Once we have outlined or written what we know about a given subject, we should find others who have knowledge of the person or event. Other family members are one of our greatest resources when writing family history. This is especially true when conducting genealogical research.

One nice by-product of writing family history is the potential it has to bring families together. Everyone in your family, from parents to second cousins three-times-removed, knows a story or a date or a name that can contribute to some aspect of your family history. Just sit down and write a short letter to Uncle Harry. You probably haven't written him since puberty (yours, not his), and he'd love to hear from you. A short note will suffice. Tell him it's been hot, the cat had puppies, and then ask your questions. You're bound to get a quick answer.

Another method for gleaning information from others is the oral history interview. There is a whole chapter devoted to oral history later in this book (See Chapter 16, **Oral History**).

Library

After we have exhausted the memories of ourselves, our friends and our relatives, we will end up having to search out written materials to fill in the blanks that are left. Actually, written documents should also be sought out to substantiate even the facts that we have already recorded.

In this modern day and age there are a multitude of places we can look for records that pertain to our lives. When searching for information on your ancestors, the most obvious are: census records; land records; religious records; wills; newspapers; family bibles; county and local histories; cemeteries; birth, marriage and death records; military records; and immigration records. (For additional information on conducting genealogical research, see Chapter 17, **Genealogy.**)

When doing research on your own life and your immediate family, the list of possible sources is almost endless. Many of these can be found in your own home, and the homes of relatives. These include, but are not limited to: birth certificates; baby books; report cards and other school records; religious records and certificates; newspapers; journals; letters; wills; insurance policies; medical records; passports; military records; employment records; tax statements and returns; pay records; photo albums, and home movies. If you've had any special hobbies, or were involved in sports, include awards, certificates, and other related documents. (For additional ideas on what to include, see Chapter 9, **Documents.**)

Although I have presented these resources, ourselves, others, and library, in the order in which they are most efficiently used, you will find times when the situation warrants the complete opposite. Imagine, for example, that you find a will (**l i b r a r y** resource) that mentions an uncle you don't remember hearing about. When you ask your mother (**others** resource) she tells you that he died when you were young, but that he played with you when you were a small child. Some of the things she tells you triggers your own memory, and you recall certain episodes and events (**ourselves** resource), which you then record in your family history.

When conducting research with others, always ask about documents they have or may know of. Get photocopies made of those that pertain to your family's history, and add them to your archives. If they have photographs, consider borrowing them and having copies made for your own files (when borrowing, be sure to return promptly).

Record-Keeping

Usually the most neglected aspect of conducting research is record-keeping. A good system is essential to efficient research. Where did you find that date? You may know today, but will you remember next year, after you've been searching for scores of other bits of information? What about the names and dates you haven't yet found? Where have you already looked? If you don't remember, you may waste valuable time looking again in places you've already searched.

There are as many systems of record-keeping as there are researchers. Experiment until you find something that works for you. One way to start is to create a file for each person in your family. Each time you conduct research on that person, whether searching documents or interviewing relatives, write down on a sheet of paper what, where, and when you looked for, and the results. Then put the paper in the file. Be sure to keep all copies of documents together.

Another reason for keeping records of your research is to prove to others that what you have written is true. Otherwise, all they have to go on is what you yourself have written (a secondary source). How do they know that you didn't just make it all up? If you keep copies of all the documents you find, and record your interviews with others, other researchers can review these primary and secondary sources and, hopefully, reach the same conclusions that you did.

There's More!

No matter how much research you've done, and how complete your story may seem, there will always be documents you haven't yet found, interviews you haven't conducted, and questions you haven't asked. Even for questions that were asked, there may have been answers not given, for one reason or another.

Always be willing to revise what you have written. As more facts become available, question the conclusions that until now you held true. Did it really happen the way you had thought? Were there other important contributing factors?

What I've presented in this chapter is only an overview to conducting historical research. For the most part, it is all you will need to complete most of the projects in this book. Genealogical research, however, is a very technical and involved science. There are many excellent books that deal only with genealogical research. I've listed some of these in the bibliography. Many give detailed instructions, and include guides which will help the novice and professional researcher alike. If you have trouble with any aspect of your research, seek out some of these books, and find other people who are experienced in this type of mystery-solving.

Whatever you do, don't let the thought of research scare you off. Many of the history projects covered in this book require little or no research beyond what you yourself already know, or have available within your own home. Even if you complete only one of the projects that follow, you will have created something that may last for generations to come, a valuable gift to those who follow in your footsteps.

CHAPTER 4
Writing

As with research, many people are uncomfortable when it comes to *writing*. One doesn't need to be a professional writer to be a good family historian, however. Anyone capable of writing a letter, or putting together a photo album can create one or more of the projects included in this chapter.

In the good ol' days, the writer's tools were the chisel and the stone. (Note: In family history, the old days were always *the good ol' days*!) Today's family historian, however, has several modern inventions that make the job much easier and less time-consuming. They are the pen, the typewriter, the computer, the tape recorder, and the camera. All you need is *one* of these to begin recording your family's history. Start now, using the tools that you have available. A thoroughly researched and penned on a napkin history is more valuable than a hardbound, typeset with color photographs history based on shoddy research and questionable sources.

Organization

Before you write your first word, you need to decide how your material will be organized. In writing history, the most obvious pattern is **chronologically**. You might begin with your birth, and continue in sequence to the present.

There are many times, however, when you might want to organize your story differently. One popular pattern is **topically**. For example, if you were writing a special study about your children, it might make more sense to discuss each child (topic) completely, in separate chapters. It would be easier to follow than jumping back and forth between children as different events transpired in their lives. Most of your writing will follow one of these two patterns, or a combination of the two.

Parts of a History

Every written history, whether a short special study or lengthy autobiography, is made up of one or more parts. The most commons are covers, title pages, table of contents, and of course the narrative itself. In addition, there are several other parts that may increase the historical value or readability of the history. Below are short descriptions of the different parts that may be included in your histories. The order in which they are listed below is also the suggested order for inclusion in your written works.

Cover – The cover of the history contains the title of the work, the name of the author, and also protects the written material.

Title Page – The title page includes the same information as that contained on the cover, and may also include the date of publication and copyright notice if not on a separate page.

Frontispiece – An important map, chart, or photograph may be used as a frontispiece.

Foreword – A statement concerning the history written by someone other than the author.

Preface – A short statement, similar to an introduction, written by the author.

Table of Cotents – The table of contents lists the names of chapters, sections, and topics in the history and the pages on which they begin.

List of Illustrations – A list of photographs, maps, and charts, with page numbers.

Chronology – A brief chronology of significant events during the period covered by the history or study.

Narrative – The main text of the history.

Appendices – The appendices consist of charts, tables, lists, graphs, statistical summaries, and compilations of details prepared by the author.

Glossary - An alphabetical list of terms used in the narrative, with definition or explanation of each.

Gazetteer - An alphabteical list of geographical place names with their locations.

Index - An alphabetical list of names and subjects referred to in the text, together with the number of each page on which they appear.

Outline

Before you start writing, it is always best to create an outline of what you want to cover. This will be your writing roadmap. Below is a simple outline of an experience you might cover in an autobiography or special study.

My First Job

I.	Why I wanted a job A. friends worked B. wanted to buy a car
II.	How I found the job
III.	The job itself A. first day of work B. my boss C. a typical work day D. pay
IV.	Quitting the job

An outline may be as simple or as detailed as you want to make it. The more you include in it, the less likely you are to forget an important event or detail. Don't be concerned with the outline's format; just get your ideas down onpaper so you'll have something to work with.

Which Person?

Before you start writing your first draft, you need to decide which person to write it in. In first person, you write from your own personal perspective, and use the pronoun "I" frequently. Letters and diaries use first person almost exclusively.

In third person, you write as an outside observer, even when talking about yourself. You use **he, she, them,** and **they** for pronouns, and never use the pronouns **I, me, myself, we,** or **u s .** Use the person that is most comfortable for you, and whichever best suits the project you are working on.

First Draft

Once you have an outline to work from, and have decided which person to write in, you are ready to start writing. As you look at the key points or ideas you have listed in your outline, write the story down on paper the same as if you were telling it to your great-grandson. By writing it like you speak, you not only pass on a fascinating story, but you also preserve your own personality in your writing.

Remember, this is only a first draft. Don't worry about mistakes, grammar, or anything else that might hinder your thought processes. Just get the story down on paper.

Format

Before you progress very far with any of the written projects listed in this book, it is helpful for you to decide what you want the finished product to look like and how it will be put together. Will it be a 6x9", 8.5x11", or some other size? Will it be handwritten, typed, or typeset? Will it be hardbound, stapled, or be fastened and bound by some other method? Will printing appear on both sides of the page, or front side only? Will there be many copies reproduced, or just one or two? (See Chapter 20, **Reproduction & Binding Methods,** for some of your options.)

Margins

The format you decide to use will dictate where your margins need to be. No matter what size and format you choose for a particular work, you need to leave ample space around the edges of the paper. The very minimum should be one inch all around, however an inch and a half is more ideal. You may even need two inches on the side where the pages will be bound. If you are going to print the final copy on both the front and back of the paper, the right and left margins should be approximately equal.

Spacing

Whether you use single, one and a half, or double spacing is largely a matter of personal preference. Some projects look better single spaced, while others are easier to read double spaced. Choose the one that looks the best to you, and don't be afraid to use different spacing for different projects. It will get boring if they all look exactly alike.

Editing

Once you've completed your first draft, you can breathe a sigh of relief; the hardest part is over. There's still alot of work to be done, however, as you'll want to edit what you've written. You may want to rewrite several times, slowly polishing the work you've created until you are completely satisfied with your efforts. It's a good idea to let someone else edit your work also, as they'll catch things you'll miss every time. They may also offer valuable suggestions on ways you can improve it.

Try not to be too critical of yourself as you read what you have written. You'll want to catch obvious typographical erros, omissions, and unclear sentences, but don't expect it to read like a Mark Twain classic. Do the best that you are capable of, and then be proud of the work which you've completed.

Final Draft

Your final draft is the pages you'll use to make *copies* for binding. The actual pages of your final draft are called originals or paste-ups, and they should remain loose, unbound, and be printed only on one side of the paper.

Since your originals won't be your finished, bound product, you may freely erase, tape, glue, cut, and do anything else necessary to make the pages "camera-ready". Drawings and photographs can be pasted in once you are satisfied with the text, and you may even move paragraphs around using this method. Rubber cement is the best adhesive for mounting both paper and photographs, as they can still be repositioned, even after the cement has dried.

P. S.

Would you like to improve your writing skills? You could take a college course or buy a couple of books on writing, but there is no substitute for learning to write than writing itself. One can't learn to write just by reading a book or listening to a lecture – it takes practice and a little conscious effort.

There are two projects in this book you can use to vastly improve your writing ability. The first is keeping a daily journal (see Chapter 5, **Journals, Diaries**). Not only will you be documenting your life for the future, but you will also gain practice by writing every day.

The second project is writing letters. There are several different kinds of letters you can write (see Chapter 8, **Letters**), and they will all contribute to both your writing skills and your family history.

P. P. S.

If you find you have *real* problems with grammar or style, there are many good books available that you will find useful.. Check the bibliography for a list of several I have found useful.

This very minute you are making history. Whether you're a professional genealogist, or a novice high school student, you can begin today to *record* history. In the pages that follow you will find many exciting ways to document your life. Just pick one, and then start it, *today* –

PART II
THE FAMILY HISTORY LIBRARY

CHAPTER 5
Journals, Diaries

The easiest project included in this book is the journal. It's easy because it doesn't really require any planning before you start, and you can complete your first entry in as little as five or ten minutes.

"My Life is Boring"

Many folks use this excuse as the reason for not keeping a journal. There are several arguments I could use against such a statement.

One. Then why not go out and do something exciting to write about? Is there something new you could do each day that would be worth writing about? Is your life boring, or are you just bored?

Two. Your life may be boring to you, but might be especially exciting and interesting to someone living somewhere else; in another culture; in another time. In our day and age I can't imagine life being more boring than it was to those who lived two or three hundred years ago. Yet the diaries of simple folks who lived then are of extreme interest and value to us today.

Three. No, your life isn't boring. Exciting things are happening all around you, and to you, every day. It's just that you are too involved with the demands of today to see and reflect upon what is really going on. Start writing, and you'll begin to view the exciting world in which we live with new perspective. Begin writing today, and you'll find new meaning and excitement in your own life. It was there all along; writing about your life just opens your eyes to it.

What is a Journal?

Recently I've heard much debate concerning the differences between diaries and journals. Personally, I believe that the two are one and the same thing. If you think "real men" don't write in diaries, keep a journal. On the other hand, if a diary sounds elegant and profound to you, by all means keep a diary.

There are many different types of journals. People write in their diaries for different reasons, therefore they include many different kinds of things. The key to successful journal-writing is finding a type of journal that you feel comfortable with; one that you will write in regularly and stick with. Don't expect to find immediate success. Writing to a non-person may feel awkward at first, but with persistence and time your diary may actually become your very best friend.

The Stone

Before you can make that first entry, you need something to write *on*. I highly recommend that you **do not** use the popular little locking diaries with pre-printed dates and limited space for writing daily entries. First of all, they never give you enough space, and if you miss writing many days you'll end up with a book full of blank pages instead of history.

There are many good hardbound books made just for journals, however. Many of them have cute titles, and they have lots of blank or pre-lined pages. You can find them in almost any bookstore. Some ledger books make good journals, too. Spiral bound notebooks are okay, but it might be too easy for you to tear out a page some time after you've written on it (this could be good or bad). Looseleaf and typing paper are only good if you are sure you will keep the sheets organized, and have them bound when you have enough for a volume. If you choose to use a computer, be sure and back up your disks and make hard copies regularly for future binding.

The Chisel

When you go to buy your book, it might be a good idea to also buy a good pen - one that you will use only for writing in your diary. It needs to be **dark**, and *permanent*. Never use pencil for a journal, except possibly for drawings you may want to include. If you make mistakes as you write, just scratch out the error, or draw arrows to sentences that should be inserted.

Felt tip markers are okay as long as they aren't the kind that will fade. You may even choose to use different colors for different days, or perhaps different moods. Be creative with your journal!

Whether you type, print, or write (cursive) is simply a matter of personal preference, each having its own drawbacks and benefits. Use common sense. Handwritten journals are the most personal, but if your writing is illegible to most other people, it would be better for you to either print or type it. Typing is the easiest to read, but the least personal of the three.

Style & Content

The easiest way to write in your journal is to think of it as a letter to a good friend. You don't need to start it with "Dear Diary," but your writing style should be comfortable and informal. A journal, like a letter, is most interesting when it's more than just a chronological list of what you did during the day or the past week. Sometimes you'll be doing good just to write a few sentences about the day, but you should always strive to include more. Think of your entry as a magazine article. How would you write about an event if it was to be published in *Reader's Digest*? Try to get thoughts and feelings into your writing. Include dialogue from conversations where appropriate. Vary your style on occassion. The more thought and effort you put into the actual writing the more interesting and valuable it will likely be.

Format

Besides deciding on the paper or kind of book your diary will be in, you need to decide what your entries will look like, and what you will include in them. If you are writing in a small book, you may want to start each entry on a new page. If you find most of your entries are filling only half a page, you may want to begin new entries a couple lines below where the last one left off.

There are only a few things that **must** be included with every journal entry. Others you may find extremely useful, especially when conducting future research. Your particular situation will warrant what should be included.

Date. Each entry should have the current date at the very beginning. I recommend writing it completely out, such as

December 12, 1987, or 12 December 1987. You could abbreviate the month, but use letters - never use numbers for the month. A date written as 3/9/88 might make complete sense to you, but I don't know whether it's March 9th or September 3rd.

Day. Not absolutely necessary, but I strongly recommend you write the day of the week following the date. You don't need to write "Today is Tuesday"; just write "Tuesday." This simple entry adds so much to your journal by placing your activities within the context of the work week around which our lives revolve.

Place. If you travel a lot, or if you find yourself away from home on vacation or a business trip, starting each entry with the name of the place you are will be helpful when you reread your diaries in the future. Like the day, complete sentences aren't necessary; city and state or country will suffice.

Weather. You could write about the weather in your entry, or you could just put a few words in the corner of the page or the bottom of your entry. High and low temperatures fit nicely up in the corners of the page, as do sunrise and sunset times if they are important to you.

Miscellaneous. There are many other things you can include in every entry, depending upon what you do on a regular basis and what's important to you. If you are a bicyclist, you may find a place at the bottom of each entry where you simply write the number of miles you rode that day. If you read a lot, you might want to write the name of a book you finished reading that day. If you rob banks for a living, you might want to write the name of the bank and how much you got away with (great source material for the years you'll have to write your story while in prison).

Number. I suggest that you number every journal entry you ever make, beginning with the first one. It may not be of much use to you right now, but it will help you in the future should you ever decide to index your journals, or cross-reference them (more about this in Chapter 19, **Other Projects**).

Illustrations. If you are at all artistic, by all means include drawings to illustrate your writing. These could be everything from caricatures of your boss to cartoons to house plans. Use your imagination.

Types of Journals

There are many different types of journals. One type, the kind most people think of when they hear the word *diary*, is a daily record of a person's main activities. It doesn't have to be written in every day, however. Some people write only once a week, highlighting the events of the previous week. Other people write only sporadically; usually only when something big happens to them.

There are many other types of journals. A hunter might keep a journal in which he only writes during and about his hunting trips. A mother might write only about her activities with her children. An executive might write about high-level meetings and decision making, and nothing else. An athelete may choose to only write about competitions and practice sessions. Someone trying to lose weight might keep a daily record of what he eats and an exercise log. You may want to keep a separate diary of dreams, written immediatly after you awaken. Trip journals are popular; they help you recall family vacations and travel. If you find yourself working for a boss who constantly harrasses you (especially if it falls under the category of discrimination or sexual harrassment) you might find a detailed and dated diary of such incidents especially useful when seeking redress.

You must decide at some point what type of journal(s) you want to keep. There is no way you could completely document everything you do every day, so either deliberately or subconsciously you must decide what it is you want your diary to be.

Getting Started

Once you have your writing materials, you're ready to begin. Many people start their journals by introducing themselves and writing a little background. Personally, I think you should forget the past, and make today's entry as if you've been keeping a journal all your life. This will make it easier for you to get started, and you can still document the rest of your life using the other projects discussed in this book.

Forgetting yesterday is especially important after you have begun to keep a diary. Most diarists who quit writing after they have already been keeping a diary for days, weeks, or even months, do so because they feel they must catch up after they have missed a few entries. Being too tired or busy to write a lengthy entry, they put it off just one more day. Before long the task becomes too big, or the writer feels too guilty, and the diary finds its way to the bottom of the drawer, never to be written in again.

Don't let this happen to you! Forget about last week, and write only about today or yesterday. There's no need to feel guilty - you can't change the past, but you can make sure you don't miss another day of writing.

Frequency

How often you decide to write is strictly up to you. Obviously, the more frequently you write, the more of your life you'll be able to capture within the pages of your journal. Many people, however, find it nearly impossible to write every single day when starting a journal. You may want to try writing once a week, with an occassional added entry on special or activity-filled days.

When I started keeping a journal I wrote once a week for a year (though I did miss a few weeks). Then one day I decided it would be interesting to write every single day, for just one week. Doing it for only one week was easy, and I decided to make it a month. Before the month was over I ambitiously determined to write every single day for a year. I didn't make it that far before I missed a day, but I did document the greater part of my activities that year. Seven years ago I started writing down (in each entry) the number of consecutive days I had written in my journal, and I haven't missed a day since. It's no world's record, but it's one I'm proud of.

When to Write

Once you've decided how often you are going to write, you must decide when, and where you will write. The end of the day is best for some people, while the day's activities are still fresh in one's mind. But if you find yourself too tired to write at the end of the day, you'd better find another time. First thing the next morning will only work if you make the time every day before you get involved in the new day. The important thing is to find a time that works for you, and stick with it.

If you are writing only once a week, choose one day that will provide you with the time and leisure to write, and write on that same day, every week. Weekends work best for some people, however Monday evening might be better so that you can include the weekend's activities. Experiment until you find a good time for you.

Almost as important as when you write is where you write. Where do you sit when you write a letter? Try the same place for starters. Writing in bed isn't any easier than eating breakfast in bed; I don't recommend either one.

Privacy

Diaries can be extremely personal records. People often write their most private thoughts, dreams, and secret desires within the pages of their diary. This is one of the many purposes of keeping a diary - to record what you would not dare share with another person for fear of embarrassment, ridicule, or rejection.

Many psychologists advocate the use of journal-writing in therapy. Valuable insights can be gained into the mind of the person who keeps a detailed journal of their thoughts and actions. Though this may be a very worthy purpose for keeping a journal, this book approaches journal-writing only from the family history perspective. If your purpose in keeping a diary is to provide a record of your life for future generations, you must only write what you are willing for someone else to read at some future date.

This doesn't mean you shouldn't write about embarrassing mistakes you may have made. On the contrary, your journal should reflect an accurate image of you and your life. This includes writing about the bad as well as the good. If you are in the midst of a divorce and spend much of your time depressed, worried, scared, and uncertain about your life and worth as a person, it would be dishonest of you to only write about the positive things that are also going on at the same time. Therapeutically it might work wonders (though I doubt it), but as an historical record it would be of little worth.

Your diary, to be valuable, need not ever be read by your own children or even during your own lifetime. It's easier to include personal thoughts and experiences if you're certain that those whom you know will never read what you have written. But just think about how you would cherish a complete, uncensored diary written by your great-great-grandmother. So what if she got married when she was sixteen, had an affair when she was twenty-three, and then was married and divorced three more times after that. I don't think you would condemn her for the mistakes in her life, and I don't think your descendents will judge you for the mistakes you made in yours either. To them your life will be a story; a wonderful true story of life and love, and in a very real sense the beginning of their own life story.

What you should try to achieve in your journal is a balanced account of your on-going thoughts and activities. If your life at the present time is mostly good, your journal should reflect that, and likewise if you are going through difficult and troubled times, it should reflect those hardships.

If you want to keep your diary private and unseen by curious eyes, you must decide how much effort you are willing to put forth to safeguard it. For most people it is enough to simply explain to family what it is you are writing and why, and that you would appreciate them respecting your desire to keep it private. Assure them that they need not fear that you are "keeping secrets" or are leading a double life; you just want the freedom to express yourself freely without fear of embarrassment.

Even honest people may be tempted to read a few entries of a diary left unattended, however, so it is best to keep them out of sight and out of reach as much as possible. Depending upon the nature of those with whom you live, and upon how personal (or incriminating) your diaries are, you may want to get a locking cabinet or box to keep them in for your own protection and peace of mind.

Family Journal

One kind of journal your family might find enjoyable is the family journal. In it you write about your family's activities, and each person who is able takes turn writing. One family member might be responsible for keeping the journal for a week, after which time it's passed on to someone else for up-keep. It's a great tool for fostering communication, as the current diarist will have to find out from the other family members what they did each day, and determine what should be included in this important family record.

Tape-Recorded Journals

A journal can be kept without ever touching a pen, pencil, or typewriter. All it takes is a cassette tape recorder, a supply of tapes, and a quiet place to record your diary. In five minutes you can include more detail than you could in half an hour of writing, and you'll also preserve your voice for posterity. The drawbacks are that, unless you transcribe your tapes, it is difficult to find particular "entries," and the tapes themselves are harder to keep and protect from damage. A combination of written and oral journals might work perfectly for you, however, and is worth considering.

Journal Summaries

If you are able to keep a daily journal for a period of several years, you'll be surprised at how much shelf space they begin to take. You'll be even more surprised at how hard it is to find that particular entry you're looking for, should you ever want to look up something. A good finding tool is the monthly journal summary, in which you write only short statements that briefly list the highlights from each day. Each paragraph gives an overview of an entire month's activities. In actuality what you create is a detailed form of chronology, and it will save you lots of time when doing research for other history projects. I suggest using another hardbound book for summaries, or use separate sheets and keep them together in a binder.

Conclusion

What I've tried to provide in this chapter is the basics of starting a journal. There are entire books devoted to the many aspects, and especially the psychology, of journals. I have listed a few in the bibliography. There are also many good published diaries which you may find inspirational. Almost everyone is familiar with the diary of Anne Frank. Even if you don't read these popular journals, you may find it helpful to scan them and read a few entries to get some ideas as to how you could improve your own journals.

In Appendix A are some actual entries from my own journal. As you will see, they are not literary masterpieces, but they each contain a little bit of my own family's history. My life hasn't been extraordinary, yet I have found plenty to write about over the years. Once you start writing, you will too.

CHAPTER 6
Photos, Movies, Videos

The most popular form of family history is the family photo album. Few households are without at least one album filled with scores of pictures of the children's birthday parties, family vacations, and holidays. Today cameras are as commonplace as television sets, with Americans taking billions of photographs each year.

Even so, there is much more that can be accomplished with pictures than simple photo albums. They can be used to create family history displays, home movie productions, and they can be used to illustrate many of your written projects. Additionally, photos need to be identified and preserved to be of use to future generations. The following sections will help you to improve your skills as a family photo-historian, and give you some ideas on how you can incorporate photography into your family history library.

People Pictures

Before discussing how pictures can be used, we need to touch on the pictures themselves. What are "people" pictures? Basically, they are photographs that document life in all of its many splendors. There is much more to life than birthdays, holidays, and vacations. Most people don't take nearly enough pictures of their family doing ordinary things. Candid photographs of kids at play; adults at work, talking, and at leisure; and families doing things together should make up the majority of album photographs.

Good family photos should record much more than just smiling faces. The best pictures are usually the ones in which the subject doesn't even know his or her picture is being taken. Prize-winning pictures are those that tell a story, even without captions. Take pictures that show your

43

home, its furnishings, the family car, and the outside of your house and yard. Get someone to take a picture of you at work, *working*.

With the simple cameras that are available today, virtually anyone can take a picture. But knowing how to operate a camera doesn't make one a photographer any more than does knowing how to type makes one a writer. Learning to take good photographs, like any other skill, requires both study and practice. Fortunately, there is an abundance of study material all around us. The next time you are in a bookstore, spend a few minutes browsing in the photography section. There are many good books on the market filled with samples of good people photographs. Magazines also offer a limitless source of examples.

In my experience, the key to having good photographs is taking lots of pictures. Don't just take one shot of a person doing something; take several. The pros take several hundred pictures just to have one or two worth publishing. Taking a few extra rolls of pictures each month won't cost you an arm and a leg, and the results might be priceless.

Finding Photographs

Your own photo albums are not likely to contain all of the photographs of possible value to your family history. After all, the pictures in your family album are probably mostly ones that you took, and there are bound to be many other good photographs of you and your family that were taken by friends and relatives, and which are in *their* albums. Additionally, photographs of parents, grandparents, and other distant relatives are likely to be found spread out all over the country.

As a family historian, you should have copies of all photographs you feel are pertinent to your family's history. All you need to do is borrow the negative for a couple weeks to have your own print made. If the negative no longer exists or is lost, borrow the print and take it to a photo lab to have a copy negative and print made.

If there are many pictures you need copy negatives made of, you may find the cost prohibitively expensive. An alternative, if you have access to a 35mm or larger camera and a close-up lens, is to make your own copies. It probably won't be of as high a quality, however it will be affordable. Unless you also have a copystand, I suggest you make the copies outdoors on a cloudy day. Use low-speed black and white film unless you absolutely have to have color.

Look at your old highschool yearbooks; you can get copies made of photographs printed in them also. If your picture was ever in the newspaper, photograph the picture with its caption. Pictures published in local histories may also be good to have if you're including information from previous generations. Be sure to get permission from the author, however, if the book is still under copyright.

Identify Your Photos

Years ago many pictures were mounted on black paper photo albums. Many people painstakingly wrote captions below each of the photographs, identifying the people, the place, and the date. Today, however, virtually all of the albums on the market consist of plastic or plastic-covered pages that give little or no room for written identification. This has become a real problem for the family historian.

The best way to mark your photographs for future identification is to have the information right on the back of each picture. I don't recommend actually writing on the paper, though. Instead, get a supply of self-adhering labels, and write on them *before* you put them on the backs of photographs. This will prevent both pen point pressure damage and blemishes caused by ink soaking through.

Try to get in the habit of writing more than just "John, age 3." Compose a caption for the picture, just like those you see in magazines and newspapers. Tell what the person is doing, and perhaps why. It will take a little extra time, but will be well worth the effort. As a minimum, you should identify each person in the photograph, the place/event, and the date.

If you take mostly slides, identifying them is a bit trickier. You must come up with a permanent cataloging system, whereby each and every slide has its own unique number. This number must be written on the slide mount. Captions are then written on separate sheets, and are keyed by the corresponding slide number. I suggest keeping all of your caption sheets together in one binder, or in several binders if you have a great many.

Organize Your Photographs

Once you have marked all of your photographs for future identification, you need to organize them. First, go through and separate the chaff from the wheat. Too many people place every picture they take into their photo albums. If you have three pictures of basically the same pose, choose the best one and put the other two aside.

Next, if your photographs are slides, you will naturally want to put your best slides in trays for viewing. For your family history, however, your should have either duplicates, prints, or both made from your very best pictures. If you have duplicates made, put the copy slide in your tray for viewing, and put the originals in plastic pages designed for holding slides. They will protect your most valuable photos, and also make it easier to find and use these pictures when illustrating other projects.

One of the benefits of using slides is the opportunity it affords to turn a group of pictures into a high quality slide show. You won't always be around to narrate who is who and what they're doing. However, you can easily create a tape recording to be played with the slides. The easiest method is to just record your impromptu narration the next time you show your slides. Then just play the tape from then on. Or, you can get fancy and write a script, dubb in music, use multiple projectors, and do all kinds of imaginative things to present a professional quality program.

Your best prints, whether made from negatives or slides, should be kept in photo albums. The kind in which the photos slide into plastic "pockets" are much preferable to albums made of cardboard pages covered by acetate sheets. Either the adhesive loses it's stickiness or else it sticks too well and the photos can't be removed without damage.

Once your photographs or slides are organized, they should be kept together in a safe, dry place. Be especially careful if you have trouble with roaches; they like pictures, slides, and negatives even more than people do, and the results can be disastrous (I know from experience!).

Negatives should also be organized into files of some sort. The easiest to use, and which also offer the most protection, are the plastic pages into which you can slide each negative strip. As a very minimum, they should be kept together, identified, and protected. Keep them someplace different than your prints. If your prints become damaged or lost, you can easily get reprints made if you've kept the negatives safe. Your not-so-great pictures should also be kept together (don't throw them away); you never know when you might need one for some unforeseen use.

Displays

The first thing I notice when I go into someone's home for the first time is the framed photographs that decorate walls, shelves, and mantles. This is family history in its most visible form. It's fun to see the changes in the adults as they age, as well as the children.

My favorite displays are those that group recent family member's portraits along with photos of their ancestors. Everyone always comments on the similarities and prominent features passed down through succeeding generations. Sometime I'd like to see a display which consists of nothing but baby pictures covering several generations of one family.

There are many ways in which family history photographs can be used to decorate one's home. Numerous small pictures in simple frames documenting the life of a family can be more effective visually than a large artsy picture or painting. They will also remind each family member of who they are and where they came from. Small framed or mounted photographs of family members and ancestors can also make nice Christmas tree decorations. Just creating them could be a fun and educational family activity.

Pictorial Histories

My favorite histories are pictorial histories. Perhaps this is because I enjoy pictures so much, and the sometimes-boring text is broken up with interesting photographs. Typically, pictorial histories have photographs on every page, and the pictures and their captions share equally with the text in telling the story.

There is no magic number of photographs that turns a history illustrated with pictures into a pictorial history. Virtually any of the projects in this book could be made into a pictorial history. I have seen several good pictorial chronologies; this wouldn't be too difficult a project for the beginning family historian. Pictorial genealogies are easy too, if you can find enough pictures of your ancestors.

Generally, all that is necessary to change an already-written history into a pictorial history is a substantial number of photographs, with at least one for each of the topics covered in the text (in narrative histories - chronologies might have only one photograph for every five to ten entries). Most of the work would be in writing captions that tie the pictures to the narrative, and then laying out the new book for reproduction.

Illustrate With Photographs

Even if an extensive pictorial history doesn't appeal to you, you should try to include some photographs in as many of your works as possible. People are often surprised at how well most pictures turn out using ordinary photocopiers. If you only print text on one side of the paper, you could copy photographs on the reverse side and then print or type the captions below. This method requires very little additional work or cost.

Preserving Your Photographs

Color photographs begin to fade after only a few years. Color slides will also begin to show their age within a relatively short time. This is extremely bad news for the family historian. Hardly anyone takes black and white pictures any more, so what this means is that virtually all of your precious family photographs are slowly self-destructing.

For the greatest chance of survival, your important color photographs should all be made into carefully processed black and white prints. Properly done, these may last hundreds of years. Color slides may be made into Cibachrome prints, which will also greatly extend their lifetime. Perhaps in the future longer lasting papers and chemicals will be created for color photography, but for now you must take added precautions to preserve the pictures you already have. Keeping them in a cool, dry place will help, and remember, keep the bugs out!

It's also good practice to make copies of all your important video tapes. Only play the duplicate tapes; that way if and when they wear out or become damaged you can make another good copy from the original. Your children will probably all want copies as they grow up and have families of their own. Keep all of your original tapes together in a safe place where they are least likely to be damaged by fire, heat, moisture, creepy crawlers, or little fingers. A little extra care here may prevent a lifetime of sorrow over lost heirlooms.

Movies, Videotape

With the proliferation of home video tape recorders, many families are finding it ever easier to document the good times in their lives. Anyone who owns a VCR can easily rent, borrow, or buy a video camera to film birthdays, vacations, and holidays. Super-8 movie cameras are also still popular with some people, and both mediums provide numerous opportunites for documenting family history.

The same rules that apply to good still photography also apply to motion pictures. Especially important is the editing process. An hour of video tape may result in only ten or fifteen minutes of good entertainment.

Those who have movie or video cameras can also create family history documentaries. You could create short ten to twenty minute segments about your family. One could focus on genealogy, another on homes you and your parents lived in, and another on schools attended. Another segment might just focus on the hobbies of family members. You could write skits and plays that portray an event from the past, such as an ancestor's arrival to America. Your only limit when creating filmed family histories is your own imagination. When created with thought and care, they are bound to be more popular than the "professionally" produced garbage programs that are aired on television nearly twenty-four hours a day. They'll be treasured by your children as they grow older, and by those who follow after them.

A Photo Gallery

On the following pages are pictures from my own family's history. Some pictures are technically better than others, but they all contribute to the story of my life. Look at these and others with an open eye, asking yourself what it is that makes them appealing, how they could be improved, and how you might also improve your own family album. Then go out and take lots and lots of pictures.

Ed Banks
(right)
taking a
break during
his Army
years,
c1955.

Lemuel Banks,
Keith's great-
grandfather

Bessie Grider (left) and her roommate, Ann Mansfield,
in Huntsville, Alabama, about 1955.

Keith holding his baby brother, Roger, in front of
the Christmas tree in Spokane, Washington, December, 1963.

Keith composed a song which he and his girlfriend, Cristi
Brown, sang at their graduation from Seoul American High
School, June 1975.

Keith ringing up a sale at Newsom Music Center in Huntsville, Alabama, where he was assistant manager from November 1976 to January 1977.

During his six weeks of Air Force Basic Training at Lackland Air Force Base, Texas, Keith spent his few free moments writing letters home to Joycelyn, April 1979.

Shortly after his birth, Nathan got to meet all of his living great-grandparents. Standing (left to right) are Ingrid Banks, Viola Wilcox, and Jerusha Grider. John Wilcox (seated) is holding Nathan, September 1979.

Keith (Kermit the Frog) and Bruce Morgan (Miss Piggy) singing "The Rainbow Connection" at a church social at Osan Air Base, Korea, 1981.

Keith, Ryan, Joycelyn, and Nathan waiting at Kennedy International Airport for Flight to Madrid, Spain, January 1982.

Nathan and Ryan trying to look cool while checking out the girls at the Torrejon Air Base, Spain, swimming pool, July 1984.

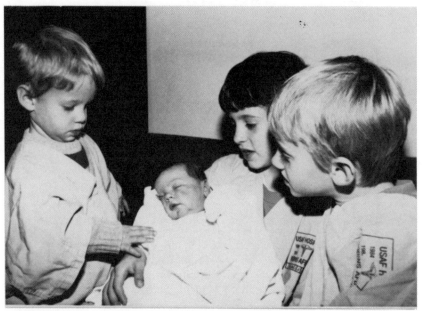

Jaron, Nathan, and Ryan getting to see their new baby sister, Chelsea, for the first time at Robins AFB, Georgia, February 1987.

Keith, Jaron, Nathan, Joycelyn, Chelsea, and Ryan posing in front of their loaded-down car as they begin their 7,800-mile trip from Warner Robins to Anchorage, Alaska, June 1987.

Nathan took this picture of his family in front of Mt. Rushmore National Monument in South Dakota, June 1987.

Nathan and Ryan are seen here trying to climb Devil's Tower in Wyoming. Ryan's foot was tightly wedged in a crack when this picture was taken, and Keith had to climb up to help pry him loose, June 1987.

Finally, after nearly a month on the road, Keith, Joycelyn, and their four car-weary children crossed the border from the Yukon Territory into Alaska. Their "Trek to Alaska" was completed later the same evening when they drove into Anchorage as fireworks exploded over the city, 4 July 1987.

CHAPTER 7
Baby, Graduation, & Wedding Books

Everyone has seen them. Go in almost any book store or greeting card store and you'll find several different books which you can buy to record your child's birth and first several years. Or you might buy another one designed to record facts and feelings about your graduation, or your wedding. They even have them now for grandparents to record bits and pieces of their own long lives. I bought another one for listing important facts concerning my estate; there are pages for listing real estate, investments, stocks (these pages are all blank, so far), important papers, life insurance policies, etc. These are all great fill-in-the-blank family history books.

For someone who wants to create a comprehensive family history library, I wholeheartedly recommend they purchase all of these different kinds of books they come across. They are easy to use, and when completed may provide information not found anywhere else. Just make sure you actually use the books once you have them; books filled with pages of blank fill-in-the-blanks won't reveal very much to your posterity about you (except perhaps that you were lazy!).

Baby books should be reviewed at least once each month to see if anything new can be added. Children grow so fast that it's easy to lose track of when exactly they did something new for the first time. Some baby books have pages for photographs, however I prefer putting our pictures in photo albums with all of our other family photos. Baby books are just one of many sources for documenting the young child's growing years.

Graduation and wedding books, because they deal only with an event (as opposed to a period of time), need to be fully filled out as soon as possible after the event. Many precious and trivial details will soon be forgotten if not written down while the feelings are still there.

The grandparent books, if you are a grandparent and just beginning to write your own history, are a good starting point. Once you've completely filled in the blank pages you will have completed your first history, and you'll have a better idea of where you want to proceed next. If you are young, these books might also make good presents for your own grandparents, however don't expect them to be as enthusiastic about writing the story of their life as you are. They might be, but then again they might not. Perhaps a better method for learning about their life would be an oral history interview (see Chapter 16, **Oral History**).

Special Occasions

In addition to graduations and weddings, there are also many other occasions which lend well to the fill-in-the-blank kind of record. Of course, you might have trouble finding a bookstore that stocks *Our Family Trip to Missoula, Montana*. You can, however, create your own custom-made fill-in-the-blank history/journal.

When I found out in October 1986 that our family would be moving from Warner Robins, Georgia to Anchorage, Alaska, I created such a book. Titled *Trek to Alaska: A Banks Family Adventure*, it turned out being a 133-page book filled with sections to document our entire trip. Since it was to be a month long trip covering much of North America by car, I wanted to make sure we always remembered the things we saw and did.

First, I wrote a short introduction telling about the circumstances that brought about this move, and a short overview of our plans for the trip. I included a table of contents, which was followed by a day by day tentative itinerary. I then included a road map of North America on which I showed our proposed route, and stops. Following the map I created a page on which I could list an inventory of everything we took with us (clothes, cameras, camping equipment, books, etc).

The largest section of the book came next, with fifty pages for a travelogue. In this section we documented every stop we made, when we entered a city or new state, and other items of interest.

Following the travelogue was budget information; how much we had available for the trip; and how much we budgeted for each day. I followed this with two pages on which we documented each day's actual total expenses, and compared that amount with the amount budgeted. Following the expense summary was a detailed expense journal in which we carefully recorded every single expense and purchase.

Information about our car came next, with a line for each day on which to record where we started the day, the current odometer reading, and a column for comments. The next section was for recording gas purchases, with columns for the date, place, miles driven, gallons purchased, price per gallon, and total purchase. Another section allowed for recording miscellaneous car expenses.

Food came next, with several pages to show where we ate every meal on the trip, and how much each cost. The following section was for recording where we spent each night, and how much lodging cost. Another section was for recording points of interest along the trip. Since we were planning on doing quite a bit of camping, I included another section to record where we camped and a little information about each campground.

With four kids and on the road for a month, I was sure that our health (physical and mental) might also be a major factor in our trip, so I included a few pages to include pertinent information. The last major section of the book was for documenting daily weather observations.

This book turned out to be a tremendous help toward preserving a record of our trip. I still wrote in my journal every day, but was able to rely upon this book to record the multitude of details that would have been easily and soon forgotten.

A similar type of book can be created for almost any major event, activity, period of life, etc. Some possibilities might be honeymoons, holidays, athletic participation, hunting trips, and reunions. You may even want to create your own custom baby book; none of the ones I've ever seen have had everything I wanted in them. Almost anything can be documented with a fill-in-the-blank type of family history book.

The best binding for such a book is the plastic comb, however any binding method will do. The pages themselves should be prepared on a typewriter or computer. Look at similar books in stores for examples of style. For the most part they are blank pages under different headings. It's better to have too much space to write information than not enough, so leave plenty of space and include lots of extra pages.

One Last Word . . .

Although the fill-in-the-blank type of book is an important part of the family history library, it has its limitations. First, like the small dated diary, it seldom has enough space to record more than the most basic information. Second, there is always information of interest which doesn't really fit any of the categories in the book. They seldom have room for recording thoughts and feelings.

More importantly, there is a tendency to rely upon such books as the only written record of an event or activity. Alone, they provide little more than a skeleton history. When supplemented with a journal or other written type of record, however, they help preserve a family's history in its fullness.

CHAPTER 8
Letters

Letters are one of the oldest forms of family history. They are also a dying form. The U.S. Postal Service is carrying more mail than ever before, however less and less of that mail is personal letters from one person to another. With television, radio, and other forms of entertainment so prevalent around us, many people have less need and find little time to commune with other people. When they do communicate, it is usually in person or over the telephone. The craft of letter writing is quickly becoming a forgotten art.

Letters as History

The epistles from Paul the apostle to the various early churches are probably the most widely read and revered letters ever written. In the centuries since they were written, untold millions of people have studied his words and tried to incorporate his message into their own lives. I doubt Paul had any idea as he sat down to write a personal letter to the Corinthians the magnitude and lasting impact his simple words would have upon a world far removed from his own. Much of what we know about the early Christian church comes from the letters of this one man.

Many other letter writers have made important contributions toward our knowledge of the world in which they lived. Letters, like diaries, tell of the lives of ordinary people: their thoughts, their dreams, their simple joys and sorrows. The letters home from soldiers fighting a long and frustrating war in Vietnam tell the true story of the conflict. The Vietnam War wasn't fought in Washington, as some historians have suggested. More can be learned about the real human tragedy of war from the thousands of letters which found their way from the horrors of the jungles and rice paddies to loved ones back home than from all the Congressional records and military documents created by this conflict.

What this means to the historian is this: **s a v e** the letters you receive and **make copies** of those which you send. Letters are as valuable as diaries and photographs. Few people would think of throwing away an old diary or photo album, yet many people end up throwing out the letters they receive, either as soon as they've been read or during the next major house cleaning.

Love Letters

Secret notes and mushy or steamy letters written by lovers to each other are usually what comes to mind when we think of love letters. I think we should also include in this category all letters written by a couple to each other, whether they fit the above descriptions, or are simply informative letters, "I miss you" letters, or the proverbial "Dear John" letter. They all provide clues to the relationship between two people.

This chapter isn't a course on how to write love letters. If you had planned on saving them for your grandchildren to read you probably wouldn't have written them in the first place. At least they wouldn't have been "love" letters. All I want to present here are some ideas on what you can do with the love letters you already have in your possession.

First of all, don't throw them out, even if they are from past relationships. The letters may not mean anything to you anymore, however they may provide information of value when conducting research for a chronology or autobiography.

Organize your love letters. Whether you have the letters both to and from you, or just the ones written to you, arrange them in chronological order and put them in a file folder or large envelope. Store them with your other important documents.

One fun possibility for a collection of old love letters is a short story. You could write a brief introduction about how the two of you (or whomever the letters are to and from) met, and the circumstances surrounding the relationship. The major portion of the story could be told by the letters you wrote to each other (either photocopied or retyped with minor editing), and with only short sections of necessary explanation added. Add a brief conclusion, make up a descriptive title, and you're done! The whole book could be completed in just a few evenings' work.

Even though they may not actually be love letters, any collection of letters could be turned into such a book. The letters written home by a Peace Corps worker in Africa would probably make a fascinating story. Try to be creative with your family history; the more you make it like something you'd read in a magazine or book the more enjoyable it will be for those who read your works.

Round-Robin Letters

One way many families have found to keep in touch is with the round-robin letter. This works especially well in larger, extended families. One package of individual letters circulates from one family to another on a continuing basis. Each time a family receives the package they remove their old letter and write a new one to go in its place, and then send the package on to the next person or family on the list.

As a family historian, you may want to consider starting such a letter yourself. Not only will it foster communication and strengthen relationships, but it will also supply you with a never-ending stream of letters for your collection. Years from now family members may come to you for copies of their old letters as they become interested in their own family's history. A bound copy of letters written twenty or thirty years ago would make a wonderful Christmas present. The possibilities are endless.

Family Newsletters

There are basically two different kinds of family newsletters. The first type contains mostly news about only one family, and is sent to friends and extended family in place of or in addition to personal letters. Many people send these kind of newsletters at Christmas tucked inside their Christmas cards. Often they are merely photocopied typed or handwritten single page letters.

The biggest advantage to such a letter is it gives one the ability to write a lengthy letter about the family to many old friends and distant relatives that might otherwise be forgotten. The negative side is that the letter is more **from** someone than it is **to** another person. Some people get around this by adding a few handwritten personal comments or paragraphs to the addressee. I think that's a good compromise.

We recently started such a newsletter for our family after moving to Alaska. I wanted it to be attractive and professional looking, so I spent some time in designing its layout and format. A portion of our first issue appears in Appendix B. We received a very favorable response from this first effort; our friends and family enjoyed reading about our (mis)adventures.

A second kind of family newsletter is similar to the round-robin letter. One person who has contact with all of the extended family, whether it be in person, by phone, or by letter, compiles a newsletter which has information about the whole family. It is then sent to each family member so they can all keep abreast of what's happening in each other's lives.

As a family historian, publishing a newsletter provides you with several opportunities. First, it keeps you in contact with other family members. You can use the letter to request information and ask for help in conducting research. You can also use it as a creative outlet for short essays and stories from your family's past. Most importantly, family newsletters, like personal letters and diaries, become valuable documents as they are preserved and organized.

Other Letters

Personal letters and newsletters aren't the only letters worth keeping for your family history. Virtually all the mail you receive, whether personal or business (excluding "junk" mail, of course), has potential value. Bills and bank statements provide valuable information for your financial history. In my archives I have a letter from the district attorney threatening me with prosecution if I didn't take out a license for a business I was no longer operating. It's an interesting conversation piece if nothing else.

If you ever write letters of complaint, letters of introduction, or even a letter to Dear Abby for that matter, be sure you make a copy for your files before mailing them. Letters from you are even more important than letters to you. They all become an important and valuable part of your family history.

CHAPTER 9
Documents

Your family documents are all of the printed records that tell something about you or your family. Some are more important than others, however they all provide a piece of the puzzle of our lives.

"Archives" is just a fancy word to describe your collection of family documents. Most people already have their most important papers tucked away in a safe place. Wills, deeds, birth certificates, insurance and mortgage papers are all of obvious continuing worth, and nobody questions the need to protect and keep them available for future reference.

Besides those documents of unmistakable future need, many other papers need to be organized and preserved for their potential historical value. The documents of ex-presidents are of sufficient volume to warrant entire libraries for their safe-keeping. There is no reason that an ordinary family shouldn't be able to organize several shelves or boxes worth of papers which represent the many activities of the family members. Report cards, awards, income tax returns, and wedding announcements are just some of the more obvious documents that should be preserved in your family archives.

These, however, represent only the tip of the iceberg of what should be kept. Anyone who has done any genealogical research knows how much can be learned from the many seemingly innocuous papers that were kept by their ancestors. Even a receipt for groceries becomes of interest as comparisons are made between the prices of today and yesteryear.

Things to Look For

The list that follows is a partial inventory of things to look for when putting together your family history. Some are

73

papers that can be kept in folders, others are books that will have to go on shelves or in boxes. Some items, such as a diploma or drivers license, you will want or need to keep some place other than in your archives. For these, make a photocopy for filing. This way, if the original document is lost or destroyed, you will at least have a copy of it.

baby books
scrapbooks
marriage certificates
newspaper clippings
deeds
birth certificates
divorce decrees
school awards
pay statements
income tax returns
leases
employment records
business records
passports
christening certificates
biographies
diplomas
school transcripts
discharge papers
donation receipts
test reports
airline tickets
accident reports
court records
sports awards
leases
medical records
household budget records
December bills, statements
vehicle registrations
recital programs
social security cards
voter registration cards
letters of appreciation
genealogies
investment records
fraternity records
adoption papers
graduation books

diaries
family Bibles
wedding announcements
wills
death certificates
obituaries
engagements
report cards
W-2s
contracts
enlistment papers
work appraisals
letters
pension documents
baptism certificates
ledger books
insurance papers
military orders
church directories
newsletters
programs (banquets, etc.)
traffic violations
loan agreements
resumes
immunization records
receipts (major purchases)
dental records
calendars (if written on)
insurance claims
business cards
drivers licenses
identification cards
powers of attorney
airline ticket copies
date books
citizenship records
photographs
petitions
wedding books

Organizing Your Archives

Once you've located all of your important family documents, they need to be organized and filed in folders. Files of documents should be kept in a safe dry place, preferably in fireproof containers. To begin with, however, cardboard boxes will do.

Similar type documents should be filed together. For example, one folder might be labeled BIRTH CERTIFICATES, and it would contain legal copies of each family member's birth certificate. One folder would hold state income tax returns, and another report cards.

The first folder in your archives should contain a master file plan. In outline form, it lists all of the files in your archives. It will aid you in keeping everything in order, and will help when deciding where to look for a particular document.

Preserving Your Documents

Most papers, like photographs, are in a constant state of slow self-destruction. This is because of the high acid content of the wood which is used to make most paper. There are papers made which are acid-free, however they cost more than untreated paper made from wood pulp. Thus, most of the documents you collect and create won't last without extra effort and care.

Humidity, heat, and light also contribute to shortening the life of family documents. So do bugs and rodents. Obviously, basements and attics are poor locations for keeping your archives.

Any documents you have which are beginning to show signs of fading or deterioration should be photocopied onto acid-free paper. Letters should be opened flat and kept loose, without rubberbands or paperclips.

If you were to try to make your collection meet archivists' standards, it would cost you a small fortune. Only you can decide how much you are willing to spend in order to help preserve your records. I expect that in the future, ways and means of preserving our documents will have progressed to the point where it isn't the major issue for historians it is today.

To those who have little or no budget for their family histories I can only recommend you do the best you can with the resources you have available. Hopefully your children and grandchildren will care for the documents which you leave to them, and like Paul's letters from centuries past, they'll last through the ages.

Bound Document Copies

Over the years you're going to need to look at various documents in your archives many times. Sometime you'll need a date or an account number, or perhaps you'll just want to enjoy reviewing the things from your past. Maybe you'll need them for researching a special study you want to write. Whatever your reasons, you're bound to refer to them again and again.

Excessive handling contributes to the deterioration of documents. There is always the chance that the paper might get torn, or have something spilled on it. The way to avoid this is to only handle **copies** of your documents. The copies can be bound together into books, and with the addition of a document list and index they will be easy to locate and use.

To create these document volumes, you first need to gather all of your documents and organize them. Once they are in folders, it is easy to take your documents to a quick-copy printer and make copies from each of them.

When I compiled my family's document volumes two years ago I found I had 780 different documents to copy. Some were small enough that I could copy two or three to a page. Others were larger than 8 1/2 x 11, so I had to reduce them slightly. Some copies, of course, required several pages. When I was done I had enough pages for seven bound volumes of documents.

Once you have your copies made, the originals can be put away and used only when absolutely necessary. Take your new document copies, and assign a number to each and every document (not page). You could use a stamp, or number them neatly by hand. I used red ink so that the number would stand out from the document, and would be easy to see when thumbing through the pages.

Once they are all numbered, divide them into stacks approximately 1-2 inches thick. These will be your separate volumes. Before you can bind them, however, you'll need to compile a document list to go in the front of each volume. This will be your table of contents. This will probably be the most time-consuming task of this project. One format to use is what is popularly used for footnotes in scholarly books and articles. Most style manuals show various examples. You could include your entire list in each volume, or just the section listing the documents found in each particular volume.

You may also want to add an index, however this isn't absolutely necessary.

The last thing to do before binding your document volumes is to design a cover. A simple title will do, however you can get as fancy as you want, possibly even using a small (or reduced copy) document to help illustrate the cover. Once this is done you can take the stacks of documents (copies) to a printer for binding. Plastic combs work best, as they allow the books to be opened flat, which will be helpful if you should ever want to make copies of a document.

In the future, make copies of documents as you collect them, and keep the copies in a folder. When you have enough pages for another volume it will be a simple matter of compiling a document list for the volume, and then gettingit bound. Just remember to start numbering where the last volume left off.

In Appendix C are examples of a cover, a document list, and documents from my own family's document volumes. This is an easy project to undertake once your archives have been organized. It should only take a few hours to make your copies, and the list can be compiled in only a few evenings (unless you have many more documents than I did). You'll then have multiple volumes of precious records ready for your family history library.

CHAPTER 10
Chronology

Chronologies are one of the most useful tools to the family historian. They provide a quick overview of a subject, an event, or historic period. Actually, everyone needs one form of chronology or another on occasion for all sorts of things. We need them for compiling a resume, for filling out a job application, and when we apply for credit. But more importantly to the family historian, chronologies provide the story of one's life in outline form.

Kinds of Chronologies

A chronology usually consists of events from our past presented in the order in which they happened (chronological order!), including the actual dates on which they happened. A job application is little more than a simple chronology of our work experience.

There is an endless array of chronologies. Go to a local bookstore, and you will find chronologies of the motion film industry, of football, of World War II, of rock music, and of the lives of famous people. Look at a history book on just about any popular subject, and you are likely to find, either in the front or backmatter, a short chronology that pertains specifically to that topic.

Even genealogy is little more than a sophisticated form of chronology. Pedigree charts and family group sheets are arranged to show the relationships between individuals, however the actual information that is recorded is the simple dates and places of a few important events in each person's life: their birth, marriage, and death.

A Short Chronology

The family historian who writes numerous special studies, conducts oral histories, writes a (auto)biography, or compiles a pictorial history will find the chronology a necessary tool for organizing her material before she actually begins to write. She will need to know when certain events transpired, and in what order. This short chronology will provide the beginning of an outline.

Obviously, a special study about your experiences as an avid hunter won't require a chronology that includes the dates your children were born or when they entered kindergarten. These dates, however, would be essential in a special study about your child's educational experiences. The date your grandfather died would likewise be appropriate in the chronology to an oral history you conducted with your widowed grandmother, but not in an illustrated account of your travels through South America.

If and when you write your autobiography, you'll also want to include a short chronology. Although it will cover many aspects from your entire life, it should only include the highlights. Three or four pages should be adequate, and definitely no more than ten. I've included a sample short chronology in the appendices.

A Master Chronology

Every time you start a new project, you'll need to search out certain dates. Imagine how easy it would be if you could go to one single book to find those dates. Think how nice it would be to have, in one single volume, all of the dates you felt important to remember. It would save considerable time spent in research on future projects; it would be just a simple matter of extracting the dates pertinent to your current project. Such a comprehensive compilation would probably be of interest in and of itself.

A master chronology is easier to create than it sounds. Once started, you'll be surprised at how fast you are able to compile the important dates from your life.

To start with, write down all of the most important events from your life, whether you remember the dates they happened or not. Include births, graduations, weddings, divorces, deaths, job changes, moves, awards, vacations, major purchases, illnesses, social activities, memories from childhood, and anything else you can think of. Don't worry about getting the events in order; at this point this is mostly a

brainstorming exercise. Complete sentences aren't necessary; just a few words to get the idea down on paper will suffice.

Next, go through your family documents and photo albums,
and see what memories they trigger. You will likely find
scores of dates and events you can include in your chronology.
If you or anyone in your family has kept a diary, they will be
able to add immeasurable detail to your rapidly growing list.

Next, add dates to your collection of events. Try to assign
approximate dates to the events you don't know the exact date
for. Some items you'll be able to come close, as in "early
November 1973," others you will be lucky just to remember
the year it happened.

Once you've asssigned an exact or approximate date to
each item on your list, you can begin putting them in
chronological order. This is a good time to expand your short
statements into full sentences. Keep them as short and concise as possible, however, as this is only a chronology, and
not a detailed history.

At this point you can continue to revise and expand your
chronology, making it as complete and accurate as possible,
or you can bind this "working copy" for reference and concentrate on other projects. You could even sprinkle it with
captioned photographs, making it an illustrated chronology.
Either way, you should update and add entries as you find new
items of interest, and as one year turns into another, and then
another.

Timetables

Timetables are similar to chronologies, with one major addition. Personal chronologies list only events directly involv-
ing the individual or family, whereas timetables also include
events of general historic interest. For example, in my
family timetables book in the year 1857 I've included not only
my great-grandfather's birth, but also the fact that the tune
"Jingle Bells" was composed. More recently, 1969 lists
man's first step on the moon right before my family's move to
Germany.

Naturally, your source of family history events and dates
will be your chronology. Getting the other dates will require a
little research, but there are several excellent sources. Almost any almanac will include a chronology of major historic
events. They may include several lists; one for politics,
another for disasters, and many others for different subjects.

One book that is more comprehensive than all the rest, including items from the arts and sciences as well as major political events, is called *The Timetables of American History*. You should be able to find a copy in the library. With this book and your own chronology, the only thing that will be missing is items of interest from local history.

For local history items you'll have to visit your local library to see what is available. Most counties have published histories, and newspapers are usually kept on file for your review also. Be sure to include population figures; they are always of interest. This research adds a lot more work to what would otherwise be an easy project. For your first draft you may want to skip local history. This is especially true if your family has moved around a lot.

There are several formats to choose from when compiling a family timetables book. The easiest is to just add these other general interest entries to your chronology, fitting them in chronological order between and among your family history entries.

A little more presentable and professional format is to list the items under headings, as is done in *The Timetables of American History*. You could arrange the entries under four columns; World History, U.S. History, Local History, and Family History. I've included a sample timetable using this format in the appendices.

Timeline

Similar to a timetable is a timeline. A timeline, however, presents the dates and information graphically on a single page. You may need to tape or glue pages together if you want to include a lot of information. It may be used to decorate a wall, or folded to fit into a book.

A simple timeline consists of a single straight line drawn across the length of the page you're using. The line is then divided equally into years, with earlier years to the left, and the present year at the other end of the line. Below the line, events are written under the corresponding year or years. You may choose to include only events from your family's history, or you could also include other events from American or world history. Look for examples of timelines in books and museums before you begin yours; they may give you ideas on what you want yours to look like.

CHAPTER 11
A Short History

A short personal history can be a fun and easy one-evening project. There are many kinds of short histories, and they come in all sizes and shapes. A resume might even be considered to be a short history. I've seen many "bio-sheets" that are excellent examples of short history, and they are usually no more than two or three pages. In this chapter I will discuss two different kinds of short histories.

The Short "Bio"

Many executives and senior officials in government and the military are frequently asked by the media and others for biographical data. The information may be needed for a newspaper story, for an information packet as part of a formal visit, or for an introduction to a speech. Or perhaps someone is just interested in that person's life. As a result of these frequent requests, people in such positions usually have a one or two-page "bio" sheet already prepared which they give out to those who request such information. The bio is usually prepared by public relations departments, and appears under an official letterhead or as a "Fact Sheet."

By way of introduction, bios usually tell what the person's present job is and their responsibilities. It then tells when and where the person was born, possibly naming their parents and telling how many brothers and sisters they have. The bio then tells where the person graduated from high school, tells where they went to college and what they majored in, and lists degrees earned.

Most of the remainder and bulk of the bio is devoted to the person's career, listing different places lived, various job positions and responsibilities, and any outstanding achievements and awards.   Finally, the last paragraph names the spouse and children.

To a family historian, short bios can be especially useful, as they provide a brief abstract of a person's life. A collection of bios for everyone in your family, bound for easy reference, would be a valuable historical document. You may not find the time to write detailed histories of aunts, uncles, cousins, or even brothers and sisters, but a short bio on each would be relatively easy to compile. Just start with your own, and then proceed to write one for each of your other family members.

Instead of the format given above, however, I suggest starting with the person's birth and tell who their parents were. How many brothers and sisters did they have? Move on to cover the highlights of their life, including moves, hobbies, education, jobs, relationships, children, etc. Unless the person moved around a lot or changed jobs frequently, you should be able to cover their life in less than two pages. In my own bio (included in the appendices) I've condensed my life into four pages; I've moved more than fifteen times. I could have compressed it further, however I felt it was more important to add a few interesting details than to save paper.

The bio format also lends itself well to short family histories. It will probably take an extra page or two, as you'll want to include information on each person in the family.

Short Story Histories

If you would like to have an autobiography, but can't find the enormous amount of time such a project requires, a short story history might be the thing for you.   It's the happy medium between a simple bio sheet and a full length autobiography.   Generally, short histories run between ten and fifty pages, and are relatively easy to research and write. This format can be used for both personal and family histories.

To write your short story, first sit down and review your chronology.   Then, choose the events which you feel need to be covered, and write a short outline. At this point you should decide approximately how many pages your history is going to be.   You will then be able to tell about how many pages (or paragraphs) each topic will need to be to fit this length.

Unlike the autobiography, in which topics are written at random over an extended period of time, the short history is best written straight through from beginning to end. Start with your birth (or before if you desire), and then continue to the present. Don't be concerned about style or detail on this first draft; just get it down on paper. You can make additions, changes, and major revisions as you write a second and final draft. You may also want to add a few pictures to your short story; they'll definitely make it more interesting for all those who read it. Design a cover, compile a table of contents, add a short chronology, and you'll be done. Short histories are best bound by saddle stitching or plastic comb.

A shorter history shouldn't take more than a couple evenings to complete; longer ones may require several weeks. You should always strive to complete any short project such as this within a month, however, as they tend to remain unfinished if allowed to take longer.

CHAPTER 12
Special Studies

Special studies cover a wide spectrum of projects. A short essay on your grandfather's military experience in World War I might be considered a special study, as would a detailed medical history of your family. Special studies are easily identified by their focus on only one aspect of our lives, and usually cover that topic in much more depth than a general history would. In this chapter we will look at some possible topics for family history special studies.

Hobbies

A fun special study to write is one that tells about a hobby of yours. You might write a special study that tells about your hobby of metal detecting; how you got started, equipment used, interesting places you have searched, and your best finds. Such a special study might be ten pages in length, require no actual research (written entirely from memory), and take only two evenings to complete.

"One Day"

A common question interviewers like to ask older people about earlier periods of their life is, "What was a typical day like?" Can you remember what your typical day was like when you were a young child? In this special study you cover in detail one of your "typical" days. What time did you get up? What did you do to get ready? What did you eat for breakfast? What time did you leave for work, and how did you get there? In detail, what did you do all day at work? What did you do for lunch? What time did you get home? What did you have for dinner? What did you do all evening? What time did you go to bed?

This could be done as an "average" day, however I think it's better when you use an actual "typical" day. In other words, choose an actual day that you expect will be typical of most days, and then record everything that you do that day. It could be done for your whole family, with separate chapters for each individual. Another variation on this theme is to write "One Week." This way you cover several different typical days, including a Saturday and Sunday.

Sports History

Were you a jock (what's the female form? jockette?) in high school or college? If so, a detailed athletic history, or your involvement in just one sport, might make an important contribution to your family history library. What was your earliest experience in the sport? What were some of your most vivid memories; your successes, and your failures? Who were your idols? Be sure to include photographs and newspaper clippings (possibly in an appendix if there are many).

Homes

A fun special study would be a history of all the homes you have lived in. You could start with your first home - the one you were born in or came home to from the hospital. Describe what it looked like, what it was made out of, and what the yard looked like. Draw a floor plan if you can remember it (or get your parents to), and tell which bedrooms were whose. How was the house (or apartment, or trailer) heated, cooled? How did you feel about this house? Where did the family spend most of their time when at home?

Create a separate chapter for each home you have lived in, addressing the above issues for each of them. Be sure to include photographs. In the appendix, include a list of the homes with their complete addresses. A chronology listing each time you moved would also be helpful.

Medical History

An extremely valuable special study is the medical history. This is especially true if your family has a history of cancer, alcoholism, mental illness, or any other affliction that tends to be passed down from one generation to the next. It can be as simple as a list of childhood diseases, illnesses, operations, and injuries you have had (with dates), or as detailed as an in-depth analysis of family hereditary traits; diagnosis and treatments of illnesses; and comprehensive account of general health over an entire lifetime.

Short History

Unlike the short history discussed in the previous chapter which covers your whole life, this special study covers only a specific period of time in one's life, and often only a specific topic during that period. An example might be your experience in the military, from induction to discharge. You could have separate chapters on basic training, job specialties, different assignments, and war experiences. Practically any short period of your life is a good candidate for a short history - high school, college, missionary experience, individual jobs, some marriages, etc.

Career

A career special study includes all of your work experience, from part-time jobs in high school to volunteer and church work, to long term career jobs. Include parental and peer influences, childhood dreams and goals, educational preparation, how you found your jobs, duties and responsibilities, promotions, pay, reasons for quitting or being dismissed, continuing education (job related), and general feelings of job (dis)satisfaction. Be sure to include a chronology in the beginning. In the appendix you may want to list addresses of past employers, and the names of supervisors. This will help you when filling out future job applications.

Relationships

A short study recounting all your past and present relationships may be fun to write. How long has it been since you thought about your first boy or girlfriend? In this study you could also tell how you got dates (what lines did you use?), what you typically did on a date (remember, your grandchildren will be reading this), and what qualities you were looking for in a spouse.

How long did these relationships last; what problems were encountered; and why did the relationships end? If you are divorced, what were your feelings about divorce before and after? How did friends and family react to your announcement that you were ending your marriage? How did you readjust to the single life?

This special study will probably be one of the most popular history projects with your teenage or grown children (if you let them read it), however your spouse may not be so understanding of your preoccupation with those who came before. Again, be sure to include a chronology. The study can be divided into several chapters for different periods or phases of your life, or you could have a separate chapter for each relationship. Include pictures if you haven't thrown them out already.

Financial History

A financial history should be a required part of every family history. Perhaps the greatest factor in influencing every other aspect of our lives is our economic condition. It dictates what part of town we live in, what kind of car we drive, what we do for entertainment, the education we receive, where we go on vacations, the gifts we give our family, the clothes we wear, and the people we associate with.

A good beginning for such a history would be with your parents; was your family wealthy, middle class, or poor, and how did you feel about your economic status? How important was money to your parents? Did your mother work, or did your father work extra jobs to help improve the family's position?

How much money did you hope to earn when you became an adult? How realistic were your goals in terms of financial rewards? What influence did finances have on your family planning? An interesting essay you could include, possibly as the last chapter, would be "What I Would Do With A Million Dollars." Don't laugh, your thoughts here will reveal a great deal about your priorities, your dreams, and the kind of life you might live if you didn't have economic limitations.

Include appendices that list annual family income (estimate if you don't have actual records), taxes paid, a loan history, major purchases (cars, houses, large appliances), credit cards, savings accounts (list end of year balances if you can), investment data, businesses operated, contributions to charity or political campaigns, and any other factors that effect your economic condition.

Religion

What part did religion have in your upbringing? What influence has it had in your adult and family life? For some people, formal religion may be totally absent in their lives, however everyone has a philosophy of life, whether they realize it or not. Even an atheist, who believes there is no God, has certain values which govern the way they live and treat others.

For members of a formal religion or church, an explanation of beliefs can be found in many sources. Of value to the family historian, therefore, is not so much what one believes, but rather how those beliefs actually influences one's daily life. Of interest would be the expectations and requirements you have had difficulty living up to or accepting, and how you resolved these conflicts.

If you have been active in leadership or teaching positions in a church, tell about these in detail. In the chronology be sure to list all significant events, such as christenings, blessings, baptisms, ordinations, callings, etc.

Vacations, Travel

Everyone likes to go back and look at photos of family trips, reminiscing about these enjoyable times. A special study that tells the story of these adventures, illustrated with photographs, would be a welcome companion on a cold and snowy day in January or stormy August night. Your family will cherish the memories which are so preserved.

One place to begin would be with your honeymoon, if you had one. Tell where you went, how you got there, what you did (remember, this should be rated no higher than PG-13), what the weather was like, and the special experiences that were worth remembering. Each trip or vacation could be recounted in separate chapters in this study, however the content is much more important than its organization. This is true with all family history projects.

Don't Stop Here

I've mentioned only a handful of the possible special studies of interest to the family historian. There are an endless number of ways in which a person's life can be organized and recounted, however. Look at the list of lists in the next chapter, and at the topics included in the chapter on oral history (Ch 16). They will provide you with many other possible topics that might be of value and interest in your own family history library.

CHAPTER 13
Lists, Maps

Lists are the easiest project, as far as writing goes, that you can undertake in compiling your family's history. They are also very popular. Go to any bookstore and you are likely to find several books of lists.

Lists provide a quick reference to many facets of your life. They are helpful when you need a certain fact, figure, or event. A book of family lists, along with a chronology, would even give a fairly complete account of a person's life without ever having to write a narrative account. Someone who finds writing difficult might want to go this route in the beginning. Reducing an account of your life to lists and chronologies makes organizing a comprehensive record more managable, even for the accomplished writer. Less time is required for researching facts and figures.

Almost every special study or major writing project can be enhanced by one or more lists pertinent to the subject. It will make future research faster, however, if you create a book of lists which includes all of the lists you have compiled. In addition to the lists themselves, all it will need to be complete is a cover and table of contents.

A List of Lists

The following list lists some lists you might want to list in your book of lists. Of course, there are many other lists not listed in this list of lists. The list below should give you some ideas on other lists that may be pertinent to your own life history and lists.

addresses lived	school teachers
jobs held	college courses
annual family income	credit cards

past loans
states visited
plane trips
cars owned
famous people met
valuables owned
movies seen
personal disasters
awards
relatives' birthdays
places visited
favorite foods
foods you hate
heroes
accidents
voting history
best friends
turning points
weight, by year
favorite possessions
skills
childhood illnesses
churches attended
organization memberships

volunteer work
countries visited
vacations
boyfriends/girlfriends
pets
books read
businesses operated
major accomplishments
newspaper mentions
wedding anniversaries
concerts attended
favorite songs
role models
illnesses
operations
fights
fears
offices held
continuing education
hobbies
favorite entertainers
immunizations
clubs belonged to

Maps

Maps, like photographs, illustrate histories in a way that no number of words can. They can be used to show exactly where you lived at any given time, and the relationship of that place to others nearby. Look at a road atlas from thirty years ago and you'll be surprised at how much has changed. Roads now exist where none were before, some small towns have all but disappeared, and others have mushroomed.

Maps can be found for just about any place on earth, and from any period during the last hundred years. You may also do well with small hand drawn maps, though take care to be as accurate as possible. Most maps reproduce fairly well, and they can be reduced or enlarged to fit your needs. Use them liberally. You may want to keep copies of your maps in your book of lists, if you compile one.

CHAPTER 14
Annual History

An annual family history is actually a form of special study (short history); it covers only a short, specific period of time. It can be an especially useful project, particularly when compiled every year for an extended period of time.

Usually when someone gets interested in writing their family's history, they believe they must start with their parents' or their own birth, and slowly and completely plod their way through the years up to the present. The immensity of such a comprehensive project overwhelms most people to the point of never even starting.

I suggest the rookie family historian begin their craft by first starting a diary or journal. That way, even if they don't ever do anything else, those who follow can reconstruct the family's past from these intimate periodic observations.

The annual history is similar to the journal in the sense that you're not concerned with your ancient past (yes, ancient – just ask your kids) – only the most recent events. It's a lot easier to remember what happened in the past year than to recall fuzzy memories from decades past.

Outline

An annual family history can be of your own immediate family, or it can be written for your entire extended family. Either way, you should develop a master outline that will remain basically intact from one year to the next. This way you will cover the same general topics from one history to the next, providing continuity. I have found the following outline to be simple and easy to work with. I will use my own family as an example.

Preface (1-2 page overview of year)
Contents
Chronology (this one year only)
Chapter I Banks family
    Home
    Church activity
    Trips, vacations, holidays, leisure
    Transportation (vehicle information)
    Finances
    Extended family
    Plans
Chapter II Keith
    Work
    Education (when I was going to school)
    Writing (hobby)
Chapter III Joycelyn
    Work
    Misc activities
Chapter V Nathan (oldest child)
    Growth & development
    Education
    Miscellaneous
Chapter VI Ryan (next oldest child)
    (subtopics for children are all the same - separate chapter
    for each child)
Chapter VII Jaron
Chapter VIII Chelsea
Photo Gallery (selection of pictures taken during the year with
    captions)
List of Supporting Documents (see Chapter 9, Documents, for
    explanation - these are the documents that were collected
    during the year)
Index

Each of the topics in this outline is further divided into
subtopics, and sub-subtopics. These may change from year
to year. For example, under transportation you may have
"1979 Horizon," "Accident," and "1986 Skylark." Under the
individuals, you may add subtopics such as "Football,"
"Hunting," or anything else that the person is involved in.

Writing the Narrative

Once you have completed your outline, you can begin writing the narrative portion, or text, of the history. Diaries make
great source material for recalling details, however most of

the history can be written from memory. For those who are able (and willing), I think it's best for the individuals in the family to write their own chapters. The children may need some help, but this gets them involved in writing family history, and makes them proud when they see the finished book.

Since this is a collective history about more than one person, it flows better when written in the third person. This may be confusing for younger children at first, but kids learn fast. Other than that, it should be kept simple, with no more than a few paragraphs for each subtopic at most.

Sometimes you may need to give a little background history in your narrative, however keep in mind that this is an annual history, and for the most part should only examine events that happened in the calendar year covered by thatparticular history. Other topics will have to be continued in next year's history. For example, if you had a baby born in February while you were writing the previous year's history, you could cover the pregnancy in the volume you're working on, but you should save the baby's birth for next year's edition.

Keep your narrative simple and concise; any topics you'd like to cover in detail can be written as a special study at another time. Your chapters should be no less than two pages in length, and no more than ten pages if possible.

If you wanted you could include appendices, maps, and the most important documents in the back of the book. You should create a title that can be used each year with the only change being the year. If you use plastic comb binding it will be easy for your children to make copies in the future after they're grown and on their own (assuming they're interested in having copies of these histories).

Looking Back

The annual history format also works well for covering earlier periods in your life, however I don't recommend you play catch-up until you've at least written last year's annual history. For these other volumes, you may want to combine several years. For example, if you lived in Wichita, Kansas from 1975-1978, that would be a logical grouping. Or if you were married once for a period of two or three years, those years might work well for you. You may want to create one or two volumes to cover your entire childhood.

One will readily recognize that this is similar to the section in chapter 12 on special studies, where one writes a short history that covers only a short period of time. The difference however, is in its organization. The annual history utilizes a highly structured format that fosters continuity from one volume to the next. A researcher may have to read several volumes to get the whole story on a given subject.

The special study, on the other hand, is meant to stand completely alone, and covers its topic entirely from beginning to end. Each special study may be organized completely different, and may be written in alternative styles.

Looking Forward

The annual history is similar to the journal. Rather than trying to write about your ancient past, you are documenting only your most recent activities. Unlike the journal, however, it is a very structured format. Beginning to write annual histories now will provide a basis upon which future research and writing can be done, whether it be an autobiography, pictorial history, or in-depth special study.

CHAPTER 15
Biography, Personal & Family

An autobiography is what most people have in mind when they think of personal history. Thousands of biographies and autobiographies are written every year, and many find their way onto bookstore and library shelves. Biographies of celebrities are almost guaranteed to be best sellers, and thus financially rewarding to their authors and publishers.

Few people, unfortunately, are willing to invest the time and effort required to create a full-length biography of themselves or their family unless they think it will make money. Imagine a library that contained a biography of every person who ever lived. What a wealth of information would be contained therein! In it would be a complete history of the world; not just the histories of countries and of wars that are taught in our schools today, but the histories of people who make up countries, and who die in wars.

Go to practically any cemetery, and there you will find all that remains of the lives of the majority of these people who came before us; large rocks with a name and two dates carved on it, and little else. How primitive! What happened between those two dates? Wasn't there anything in their long lives worth remembering, and worth passing on to their children and grandchildren?

Of course all of the projects presented in this book contribute to the record of one's life. But the biography, whether written by oneself or by someone else, provides in one volume an overview of a lifetime of learning, joy, sorrow, achievement, tragedy, failure, and success. At some time or another everyone should prepare this account of their life.

Writing a biography, whether your own, your family's, or of someone else's life, isn't as hard as you might first suppose.

The following sections will explain the steps in making a biography a fun and underwhelming project to undertake.

Outline

The first step in writing a comprehensive biography is to create an outline. This first outline should be very simple, dividing your life into several distinct periods. They might be: early childhood, teenage years, young adult, middle age, and retirement years. Or, if you have moved around a lot, you may divide your life by where you lived. If you have been married five times, your adult life could easily be so divided. Turning points make good starting or ending points for each new epoch in your life.

Once you have this simple outline, take a blank sheet of paper and use one period of your life for a heading. Prepare other sheets likewise for each period of your life. You could use a spiral bound notebook for this, or use looseleaf sheets in a three ring binder. Keep them together, however, so they don't become lost.

Brainstorm

At this point you need to try to recall the major events, or episodes, of your life. Under the appropriate heading on the pages you have just prepared, write a word or two - just enough to jog your memory for later recall. Don't try to get them in order. Whatever you happen to think of, write it down on the next available line before the memory slips back into the recesses of your mind.

You will often find that one memory triggers another, and you'll be surprised at how much you are able to recall in a very short period of time. If you have already written a chronology (which I highly recommend you do first), read it to help jog your memory. Look at the different lists found in this book; they will also trigger some past experiences. Other memory sparkers are high school yearbooks, photo albums, scrapbooks, newspaper clippings, report cards (for recalling classes, teachers, and special school experiences), diaries, and documents found in your family archives.

I recommend you spend at least several days on this brainstorming activity. Keep a small notepad handy for jotting down thoughts as you engage in other activities, whether they be working, playing, travelling, or shopping. Memories are as likely to surface while you're in the shower as when you're sitting at your desk - be prepared.

Organize Your Memories

Once you have several pages full of brief notes representing a lifetime of memories, it's time to organize your material. The simplest way to organize your life history is chronologically. Start with your birth, and continue with each memory in the order in which they happened. After all, this is the way life occurs.

It might be more interesting and easier to follow, however, if you present your memories by topic. You could include your entire work history in one chapter, and memories about good friends in another. Your own life experiencs and personal preference will dictate how to organize your own personal history.

Whichever you decide, prepare an outline that includes each memory in the place you want it to appear. You can change, add, delete, or completely revise it as you progress with your writing. Some people prepare notecards with a title for each memory on it; others put the titles on blank sheets of paper for future writing.

Write an Episode

The actual writing of a biography isn't difficult. Pick any one of your topics, and then write a few paragraphs about that particular episode in your life. It might take several pages, or it might take only one or two paragraphs. Tell the story simply, as if you were writing it in a letter or diary.

Once you've completed a first draft of this episode, file it away, either in a notebook or folder. Pick another topic, any one will do, and then write about it. Try each day to write at least one episode; you'll be surprised at how rapidly the story of your life comes to life in words that all your posterity may enjoy.

Research

You will find that you'll be able to write most of your history completely from memory. There will be some details however, and some early childhood experiences that will be beyond your own personal recall. To help with dates, names, and places, there is no better source than a diary if you kept one. Other sources to check are your family archives, high school yearbooks, and old letters.

To help with your early childhood you will need the help of parents, grandparents, aunts, uncles, and perhaps older brothers and sisters. You could just call them on the phone or ask them questions in a letter, however an oral history would be much preferable (see Chapter 16, Oral History).

Editing & Rewriting

Once you've written the first draft of all the separate episodes that have made up your life, it's time to tie them together and polish your writing. At this point, it is best to start with the beginning and continue through your book in order. You will want to make the beginning interesting, and each topic should transition smoothly into the next. This can only be accomplished by rewriting your history in the sequence you have chosen for its final form.

Once you have completed this second draft, you should let someone else read and edit your work. In fact, I would recommend you let at least two people edit your manuscript; one could be a parent or someone else familiar with your whole life; the other could be a friend, acquaintance, or co-worker who would pay more attention to grammar and style than to the actual story itself.

Before writing your final draft, decide which pictures you'd like to use to illustrate your story. They could appear throughout the text, or grouped together in one section and printed on good paper for better reproduction. You might even decide to make this into a pictorial history if you have enough photographs and want to go that route.

You also need to decide what you want to include as front and backmatter. As a minimum, include a table of contents and a short chronology. You may also want to include in the appendices several lists you have compiled, such as addresses and schools attended. An index will make it easier to find certain facts or stories.

Final Draft

Once you have edited and rewritten your work to your own satisfaction, and have compiled drafts of front and backmatter, you should be ready to prepare a final draft for reproduction. If you don't own one, you may want to rent an electric typewriter for a week to put into form this important document. It will be well worth the small cost to be able to have a professional-looking product. Other alternatives are computers, word processors, a typing service, or professional typesetting. See chapter 20 for a detailed discussion of different methods of reproduction and binding.

Family Biographies

Most of the discussion in this chapter has been centered around autobiographies. The same rules apply however, when writing someone else's story or when writing a family biography. In the latter case you will want to focus on the family as a unit and its activities, though you could have separate chapters that concentrate more on each individual in the family.

Sharing Your Story

Having invested many weeks or months of your life in this project, you should be willing to share your story with the other members of your family. Perhaps it will inspire them to write their own history. You should have enough copies printed for each family of your extended family, and each individual in your immediate family. They will enjoy your story no matter how simply it is written and reproduced. The other projects in this book may cover your life in different and important ways, but none will be as popular and as likely to be passed down through the generations as a comprehensive biography.

CHAPTER 16
Oral History

Oral history is mankind's oldest, and most popular form of history. Long before men thought to carve their stories onto tablets of stone, they gathered their children around them and recounted tales of adventure which had been passed down by their own parents, and their grandparents before them. In some primitive cultures today, oral history is still the *only* history.

Can you remember the stories told by your parents to you as a young child? How about the one: "When I was your age I had to walk five miles to school through snow up to my knees when it was twenty below zero outside." Or, "When I was a little girl I had to make my own clothes, and we only got one present each at Christmas."

What stories have you told your children about your own life? How many times have they asked you "Tell us again about the time you . . ."? Everyone likes to hear stories. This chapter will show you how you can preserve these oral histories so that they won't be forgotten. Even the voices that spoke them will be preserved, long after the story-teller has passed on.

Oral histories relate past experiences in ways no carefully prepared written record can. First, they add detail and spontaneous thoughts and observations that might not be included if the storyteller was preparing a written account. They also record emphasis and other verbal clues that enhance the story. And in oral histories conducted using videotape, mannerisms and many non-verbal gestures contribute to the telling and understanding of the saga.

Equipment

You don't need expensive equipment to record oral histories. An inexpensive cassette tape recorder will probably do just fine. One with a built-in microphone will be adequate, although you might find a plug-in mike gives a little bit better quality recording. Make sure you can plug it into a wall outlet; battery operation should be avoided if at all possible. You may need to have a short extention cord to be able to position the tape recorder and microphone where they will best pick up the interview. In addition, you may find an earplug or headphones will help when it comes time to transcribe the tapes (if you choose to do so).

When it comes to tapes, don't ever buy cheap bargain brands for your oral histories. They don't need to be hi-fidelity, but they do need to be high quality. As for length, I've found 90-minute tapes to be the best. This allows for 45 minutes of recording on each side.

Prepare for the Interview

No good reporter goes into an interview without knowing something about the person they are interviewing, or without having mentally prepared some possible questions. Neither should you. Find out some things about the person's life from other people if possible. In your interview you'll want to focus more on the hows and whys than on the whos, whats, and wheres. Facts and dates are important, but they may be available from different and multiple sources. How this person felt about an event, or about a person, however, can only be told by that one person.

I believe in having a list of questions already prepared before the interview begins. You don't need to ask every question, and you may rephrase the ones you have and add others as you go. However, having the questions in front of you will help you to remember all of the areas you wanted to include, and will keep the interview on track.

Don't plan on covering a person's entire life in one sitting. Most interview sessions should be kept under two hours; anything longer is too tiring for both the interviewee and the interviewer. You may want to schedule several different sessions, each covering a different period in the person's life. For the purposes of your family history, you may be only interested in one short period of that person's life, or just a particular experience they shared with someone you are writing about.

112

At least a few days before the interview it's good to give the interviewee a list of topics you would like to cover in the interview. This will help them prepare by giving some advance thought about the past events in their lives. Don't give them the actual questions however, as this might result only in carefully prepared answers to your questions.

Interviewing Techniques

The craft of interviewing is an art in itself. With a little practice, though, you should be able to master the basics sufficiently to produce interesting and informative oral histories. You may want to try practicing with someone in your immediate family, using the tape recorder. Conduct an oral history with your spouse, covering their childhood. Not only will you get practice in interviewing, but the tape you create will be an actual oral history worth filing in your archives.

When conducting an oral history, it's usually best to do the interview in the subject's home. You'll want them to feel as much at ease as possible. Also, this interview should be conducted in private; not in a room likely to have uninvited visits by children, spouses, or friends. Make sure there won't be outside noises and distractions; never sit in a squeaky rocking chair. When you listen to the tape, you'll be surprised at the sounds your recorder picked up that you didn't even notice during the interview. Be absolutely sure you turn off the television or radio.

Place the tape recorder where it is close to you so that you can monitor its operation and turn over or change the tapes when needed. Place the microphone on a table or some other stationary object where it is approximately equal distance between you and the other person. Once it's in place, be sure to conduct a test to ensure that it is working properly.

At this point you are ready to start the interview. Turn the tape on, and after a few seconds (to get past the tape's plastic leader) start the interview with a statement such as "This is Sally Jones, and I'm interviewing John Wilson in his home at 1345 Main Street, Williamsburg, Illinois. Today is July 13th, 1987." Proceed then to ask your first question.

Your first questions should be simple ones that you know the interviewee will enjoy answering. You might ask them about their parents, about favorite hobbies, or anything else that will get them talking and feeling comfortable. You should save questions about personal or unpleasant experiences until later in the interview.

As mentioned before, your questions should focus on the how and why of an event or experience. For example, "When did you move to Texas?" might get you a date you were needing for your history; on the other hand, "Why did your family move to Texas?" could provide background on your grandfather's job, or a host of other things. Limit the questions that can be answered with only a word or two, and concentrate more on essay-type questions.

Be sure to let the other person do most of the talking. This is not the place for your own thoughts and experiences. More than anything, really listen to what the person is telling you. They'll be able to tell if you're genuinely interested in their story, or just trying to get a bunch of words on tape.

Long pauses in normal conversation make most people feel uncomfortable, but in the interview they are signals to the interviewer. The pause might mean, "I'm through answering this question," or it might mean "This is difficult to talk about right now." The person may just be thinking for a moment how to phrase his answer, or they might be about to add an interesting anecdote to illustrate something just said.

Avoid the tendency to jump right in with another question when you hear a pause. Give the person at least five or ten seconds to continue their train of thought. You may want to rephrase their last answer in the form of a question if you feel they haven't concluded their story. If they had said "My dad was never the same after that," followed by a lengthy pause, you might ask "You said your dad was never the same after that?" They might then explain **how** their dad was different.

Sometimes you may want to save such a question until later in the interview, especially if the person is having difficulty talking about it. You might even say something like "Let's come back to this later." The person will appreciate your care and understanding, and will be more likely to confide in you than if you throw out questions without regard to their personal feelings. Such cheap journalism is a staple on the evening news, but has no place in family history.

Always keep an eye on your tape recorder. When the tape comes to an end, it is alright to interrupt the person by saying "Just a second while I turn over this tape (or put in a new tape)." Start it running again as quickly as possible, and then get the person talking again by reminding them of what they were saying when the tape ran out.

Watch for signs of tiring on the part of either one of you. As soon as one person begins to lose interest in either listening or talking, it's time to end the interview. Trying to go beyond this point might do more harm than good. First, you're likely to get shorter (thus less informative) answers to your questions. Even worse, the interviewee might not be too eager to do this again in the future if it seemed to them to take too long.

When the interview is over, label each of the tapes with the name of the person interviewed, and the date. Number each side of the tape(s) in sequence through the entire interview. Thus, the second side of the first tape would be numbered 2, and the first side of the second tape would be numbered 3, and so on. Store them in their protective cases, and never leave them in the car's glove compartment or trunk during summer.

Confidentiality

Always be completely up-front and honest about your intentions for conducting an interview. The person you are questioning might wish that nobody else hear the tapes while they're still alive. Respect those wishes. Just make sure you both understand and agree upon how the tapes will be used. You may even want to have a short written agreement, signed by the both of you. This is especially true if you are considering publishing some of the comments made in an interview.

Tape Storage

Your oral history tapes are priceless heirlooms. They should be protected as such. Keep them together in some kind of tape storage case, and out of the reach of children. An oral history tape from an interview I conducted with my grandfather a short time before his death was damaged beyond repair by one of my young children – I learned the hard way to keep them put up high. It's also a good idea to make copies of your tapes, just in case one does become damaged. These copies can also be edited, should you want to cut out breaks or unimportant chitchat that is on the original tape.

Transcribing

A transcript of an oral history provides a written record of the interview. For research purposes, they are much easier to use than the original tapes. If the transcript includes a table of contents or index, a person can go immediately to the section that interests them and read the words which were spoken.

There is no mystery to the process of transcribing a recorded interview. It's just a simple matter of listening to the words that were spoken, and then writing them down on paper. It should be done as soon as possible after the interview, as your own memory of the conversation will aid in recalling difficult to hear or understand words.

When transcribing, you don't need to write down every "uh," or "you-know." You might even want to clean up poor grammar that is distracting when read, however you don't want to edit too heavily. You may want to break up run-on sentences, and separate lengthy monologues into paragraphs. At the end of a tape side you should indicate this by writing something like **End of Side** 3 on a separate line. This will help you locate something on tape should you want to hear the actual words.

After you transcribe a tape, it's a good idea to let the interviewee edit a **copy** of the transcript. Tell them they are free to delete, add, or change anything in the transcript. They should be encouraged to clarify statements that are unclear, or reword sentences to better portray the ideas they had intended. They may have had other thoughts on the subject after the interview, and they should be encouraged to add these additional feelings or observations.

From this final edited copy of the transcript, you should write a final draft. Include a table of contents that tells the general topics covered and where they begin. A short chronology of the person's life would also be useful. You could illustrate the transcript with photographs – try to have at least one photograph of the person at the beginning of the interview. Include lists that may be appropriate as appendices. An index will also help if you want to find something in the future. I've included an excerpt from an oral history my wife did with my parents in Appendix G. You may want to use it as a guide to style.

Other Uses

Besides being interesting all by themselves, the material you've recorded in an oral history can be used to illustrate many other types of histories. Actual quotes add to the authenticity of biographies, and make them more interesting to read.

Oral histories also tend to raise as many questions as they provide answers to others. When reviewing a tape or transcript, ask yourself what other questions you might ask on a future interview, or who else might be contacted for information.

Finally, oral history can be used for your own personal history, in the form of an oral biography. Follow the steps listed in the chapter on biography up to the point of actual writing. Then, sit down at a table with the tape recorder on and begin telling your story, using the outline you've prepared to lead from one topic to another. This is a good alternative if you're a much better talker than writer.

CHAPTER 17
Genealogy

To the uninitiated, the word genealogy often conjures up images akin to those created by other foreboding – **o g y** words, such as microbiology, archeology, geology, and seismology. Genealogy, however, doesn't require the years of education and study demanded by these other disciplines. And unlike most of the other projects discussed in this book, genealogy doesn't even require any writing ability.

Genealogy is the study of, or search for, one's pedigree. Or to put it in Biblical terminology (another -ogy word), John begat Tom, who begat Lisa, who begat Bill, who begat Fred, who begat Mary, who begat Diane, who begat Mike, who begat Harold, who begat me. In its simplist form, that's about all there is to it. At some point however, you may want to find out who begat John. That's when the real fun (and work) begins.

Getting Started

When completed, most genealogies consist mainly of filled in charts and forms. The charts help organize and present the information in a format that is easy to use and understand. There are two main kinds of forms: **Pedigree Charts** and **Family Group Sheets**. I've included samples of these forms in the appendices. Additionally, a genealogist may use several other kinds of forms to aid in record-keeping.

If you have little or no genealogy experience, I suggest that you visit several local bookstores and examine the fill-in-the-blank genealogy books that are available. Buy one that has lots of blank charts in it, but don't be too particular. Every genealogist has their own way of doing things, and you won't really know what suits you until after you've spent a great deal of time with it. Right now all you need is something to help get you started.

Pedigree Charts

Pedigree charts show who begat whom in one's family. They are the ones that often resemble a tree, with each succeeding generation branching out further into the past. Begin by filling in your own name and birthdate, and any other information called for under your name. Then write down the names and dates for your father and mother, your grandparents, and great-grandparents. Go back as many generations as you can, writing in pencil the names, dates, and places you aren't exactly positive about (including spelling). Depending upon your memory and the number of generations included on your chart, you may need to continue your lines on other charts. If you don't know a maiden name, just write down the first name.

Family Group Sheets

Family group sheets include information relevent to individual families, such as children, birth, marriage, and death dates, and names of spouses. The name of each man and woman on your pedigree charts should be included on two different family group sheets. On one, they will appear as a child with their brothers and sisters. At the top of the form will be the names of their father and mother. On the other family group sheet they will appear as either the father or mother, and the form will include the names and dates for their spouse and children.

Create a family group sheet for each couple on your pedigree chart, and fill in as much of the information as you are able. Once you've exhausted your own memory you'll be ready to begin some detective work to uncover the information needed to fill in the many holes and blanks that remain.

Individual Record Sheet

Each individual found on your pedigree charts and family group sheets should also have his or her own individual record sheet. This record documents where you found the names and dates you have written down, and also includes places you've looked for information, even if you didn't find anything there. This will help prevent you from duplicating research later on. No matter where you got the information, be sure to write it down; otherwise you'll soon forget where that important name or date came from.

Research

The principles of family history research discussed in chapter three apply equally well to genealogical research. There are some sources especially useful to genealogy worth mentioning here, however. By following the order of research presented below you might possibly save yourself thousands of hours of research time, and perhaps thousands of dollars as well.

If you have filled out your pedigree charts and family group sheets with what you know, you have already completed the first phase of research. Now it's time to find out what **others** know. Let **e v e r y o n e** in your extended family know that you are researching your family's genealogy. Not everyone will be able to provide you with a name or date, but it's very well possible that someone will know of another, perhaps a distant cousin, who has also done some research into your family's past. You may be one of the lucky ones who find that most of the research has already been done for you.

Even if you aren't quite so lucky, you'll soon know who in your family knows the most about your ancestors. Try to enlist their help; genealogy is a family affair, and the more people involved the more fun it will be. Be specific when you ask for information. "Tell me what you know about our ancestors" will most likely get you nothing. On the other hand, "What was the maiden name of your grandmother Jones," will usually get the information if the person knows it.

Once you've queried those who are most knowledgeable, and have updated your charts and forms, make copies of your pedigree charts for all of your relatives. They will be excited to learn more about their own heritage, and may be able to provide a missing name or date. Even if some of your relatives express little interest in the beginning, keep everyone regularly informed on your progress. A distant relative may tell someone else in your family of your work, someone that may be able to furnish you with the information you're searching for.

Before you progress far into your research, you need to find out if someone else has already found some of the information you're looking for. There is a good chance that some research has been conducted on at least one of your family lines. Genealogy has been a popular hobby in America for more than one hundred years, and especially in the last ten years since Alex Haley's *Roots* was aired on television.

Look at your pedigree chart. As you go back in time, each generation has twice as many family names as the succeeding generation. You have four grandparents; eight great-grandparents; and you have sixteen great-great-grandparents. If you could count all of the descendents of those sixteen great-greats, there might be more than one hundred distant cousins you and your close relatives have never even heard of. Perhaps one of them has taken an interest in their family's genealogy (and yours). You need to find out before you waste precious time and money duplicating research that has already been done.

Libraries, Genealogy Societies

There are several good sources available to you, many locally, for helping you find out what research has already been done. They will also help guide you in conducting original research that has yet to be done. For many people, it's possible to conduct almost all of their research without ever leaving town, no matter where in the world their ancestors came from.

The largest genealogy library in the world is located in Salt Lake City, Utah. It has millions of pages of microfilmed civil records from all over the world. It's no longer necessary to go to Germany or Sweden to find birth and death records for your ancestors; there's a good chance it's on microfilm in Utah! This library also has many thousands of genealogies, listing more than 70 million names that have been submitted for permanent safekeeping. These files are also available to researchers. For a small fee, library staff workers will check one of the names on your charts to see if they already have that person listed in the library's holdings.

This library is operated by The Church of Jesus Christ of Latter-day Saints (Mormons), and they have branch genealogy libraries located in almost every average-sized city in the United States. These libraries are open to the public, and are in fact used more by non-Mormons than by LDS church members. Through these branch libraries you can order any of the microfilms located at the main library in Utah, which you can then view on the branch library's microfilm readers. Staff workers are available to help guide you in your research.

The LDS branch libraries also have all the charts and forms you'll need for dealing with the main library in Salt Lake City. To find the one nearest to you, look up **Latter-**

Day Saints in the yellow pages under **Churches**. Call to find out the hours they are open; it's normally just a few hours several evenings each week.

Another local source you should check is the public library. Many have extensive collections on local history, including a good deal of genealogical data. Be prepared to spend a lot of time at the library however; most of this kind of material is not available for check-out, and must be used only in a designated area.

Finally, look up your local genealogical society. They may have publications and other services that will immensely aid your research. They will be able to tell you what other sources and services are available locally.

Remember, in this early stage you should be trying to find out what research has already been done. Only then should you begin to invest the enormous amount of time (and possibly money) required to conduct original research.

Where To Go From Here

Genealogy research can be rewarding and fun; it can also be extremely frustrating. Every family history should include, as a minimum, a pedigree chart showing four generations of ancestors. How far you decide to carry your research beyond this point is up to you.

For some people, genealogy becomes a lifelong hobby; they wouldn't think of paying someone else to experience the joy of discovery that awaits them in courthouse basements, dusty attics, and voluminous libraries. Get your own fill-in-the-blank genealogy book, and see where the search leads you. Genealogy is one of the few detective stories open to participation by all people who like mysteries, and every family is different. You'll be surprised at how much fun it can be.

CHAPTER 18
Who's Who In Family History

What was the name of your high school guidance coun-
selor? Did you like her? What do you remember about her?
How about your first boss? Do you remember what his name
was? What about the name of the family that lived next door
to you before you moved into your new home?

Some people remember names better than others. Some
people, like me, don't remember names at all. I can recall
faces, but they're all nameless faces. Even if your memory
for names is excellent, your children may have trouble
remembering who's who when they read your written histories.

Almost everyone has seen or heard of *Who's Who in
America*. There are literally hundreds of different **who's who**
style books. There is one for nearly every field of endeavor,
and for almost every state and large city. For most people
it's an honor to be listed with other prominent people in their
field of specialization. Being listed appeals to one's ego, but
these books are also a great help to researchers. Otherwise,
libraries across the nation wouldn't spend the thousands of
dollars required to acquire the most popular collections.

A **Who's Who in Family History** is an easy project to
compile, even for people like me with poor memories. This
who's who book is unique to your own family, or your own life,
and lists the names of people who have interacted with you
during your lifetime. You may even want to include the
names of ancestors, idols, heroes and the like.

Compile Your List of Names

To begin your who's who book, sit down at the table with
pen and paper, and just start writing down names along the
left-hand side of the paper. At first the names will come to
mind faster than you can write them down. Be sure to list all

of your relatives. When you've written all that come quickly
to mind, go back to your early childhood and think about each
period of your life up to the present. The following list may
help trigger your memory:

doctors	babysitters
neighbors	friends
enemies	teachers
boyfriends	girlfriends
pets	co-workers
bosses	clergy
grocer	mailman
teammates	parents' friends

Once you've gotten this far, review your family archives to
see what names they may add. Be sure to look at school
yearbooks, photo albums, and scrapbooks. You won't be able
to recall the names of everyone; some on your list will only
have first names, others will be only last names. You'll probably think of more names tomorrow and the next day; some
you won't recall for months or even years. You never know
when a name might come to you, but when it does be sure to
write it down immediately on something handy before it slips
back into your subconscious mind. Add it to your who's who
that same day, no matter what format or stage of writing it is
in.

After a few days or weeks of brainstorming, you'll realize
you have recalled most of the names that are going to come
easy to you. It's now time to turn your list into a who's who.

Alphabetize Your List

The second stage of developing a family who's who is to
put all of your names in alphabetical order, by last name. For
those people for whom you've only remembered the first
name, you have two choices. First, is to add their first name
alphabetically amongst the last names; thus Janet might fall
between Jamison and Johnson. Your second option is to
create a section of the book just for first name people, with
those names in alphabetical order.

Biographical Data

The last stage of writing this who's who book is to tell
something about the people you've listed. This can be either
easy or hard, depending upon how detailed and sophisticated

you want to make it. It's best to make it as simple as possible for your first draft, and then add more information later if you want.

Following each name, write just one or two statements (not necessarily complete sentences) summarizing the person's relationship to you. Examples might include: boyfriend, Mar-Apr 1962; math teacher, 8th grade; next door neighbor, 1966-69; or eye doctor, 1974-79.

After you've completed this for each of the names on your list you'll probably want to add a little bit more information for *some* of the people. You might tell a little bit about the person, or more specifics concerning your relationship. The average entry should be no longer than three or four sentences. In any case, no entry should be more than one long paragraph. If you want to write more about the person, save it for a special study; the who's who book should contain only short, concise entries for easy use as a reference book.

Finishing Touches

Before rushing off to press with your completed manuscript, is there anything else that might add to the quality of this book? How about photographs for some of the people? They could be placed with the written entries, or placed together in a separate section of the book. A short chronology might even be useful, although less so than for other projects. If you have more than one section in the book, you should include a table of contents telling what each section is, and what they contain. Also, include at least a dozen blank pages in the back of the book for updates.

Update Regularly

Even after you've printed and bound your who's who book, it isn't finished. You're always meeting new people, making new friends, working for new bosses. Like the chronology, it needs to be brought up to date at least once a year. Use the blank pages you bound in the back of the book until you have enough new entries to warrant a complete revision.

CHAPTER 19
Other Projects

In addition to the dozens of ways for preserving memories already discussed, there are scores of other fun projects that can make a contribution to your family's history. Some are writing projects, others are more craft oriented. Look over the projects which follow to see what appeals to you. They may even give you ideas for other projects that haven't been covered in this book.

Calendar

There are several different ways a family history calendar can be made. The simplest is to just take a store-bought calendar and add significant dates from your family's past. If you or someone in your family is creative, however, it's more fun to create such a calendar from scratch. You could use an old family photograph to illustrate the calendar, or perhaps create drawings depicting scenes from the lives of ancestors. There are many ways and formats you could utilize; use your imagination. If you find it difficult to keep a diary, you might also try using a calendar to document your comings and goings. An entry or two each day will go a long way toward preserving a record of your busy life. Small pocket calendars work especially well for this type of record.

Cookbook

Every family has their favorite meals and dishes. Why not create a cookbook that includes the recipes for all of your favorites? It will make cooking easier, as all of the recipes will be in one book. Copies of such a cookbook would also make wonderful presents for your children when they move away from home.

First Person Stories

Look in practically any magazine and you'll find a first person narrative someone has written about an event in their life. Everyone likes to read about other people's experiences. Why not write short essays about your own life experiences? Thousands of people are getting paid good money every year to write such stories; why shouldn't you reap some of the spoils? Small local newspapers are an especially good market for first person accounts about your childhood or your grandparents. Even if they're never published, your family will love reading your short stories.

Gazetteer

A gazetteer is a dictionary of place names. This is especially useful if many of the places in your family's history are small towns unfamiliar to most people. Entries should also include the cemeteries ancestors are buried in. The format should be similar to that of the who's who book, with only a few short sentences telling exactly where the place is located, and perhaps its population (towns - not cemeteries!). You may even want to include a section of maps in the book, pinpointing where these different places are.

Home Finder

How many times have you had to give someone directions to your home? Did you draw them a map, or did you just tell them to turn left at the third light, go about three miles and turn right by the fire station, turn left at the second stop sign, and your house was the eighth house on the right? In just two or three pages of carefully prepared directions, you could provide your future guests with a fool-proof home finder.

Find a easily located landmark, perhaps the edge or center of town, that everyone coming to visit you will have to drive by; this will be your starting point. Drive there, and take a portable tape recorder. Set the tape player to "record," and begin driving back to your home. Narrate outloud everything you see along the way, and be sure to mention every stop and turn. Watch your odometer, and tell how far you've traveled between certain points.

When you get home, write down the detailed instructions to your home, based upon your own observations noted on this trip. Finally, create an accurate map to accompany your written instructions. Your finished home finder should be 1-4 pages in length. Make lots of copies so that you'll have one available to hand out to the next person needing directions. Be sure to file at least one copy in your archives for your family history.

Comprehensive Index

Many of your written projects should include indexes in them. These will aid in quickly locating the names, places, and events you've written about. If you end up with many books in your family history library, you may want to compile a comprehensive index to all of your works. When looking for information, such an index would lead you to all references to your subject. Looking up your child's birth, your index would lead you to journal entries, your chronology, special studies, autobiographies, documents (birth certificate, announcement, etc), oral histories, photo albums, and any other place where the desired information is located.

Quilts

Patchwork quilts are a fun project the whole family can take part in. One quilt might be centered around your ancestors, with their names and birth dates embroidered on separate squares. Or you might get everyone in your extended family to make a square of their own design, also embroidered with their name. You could then put the squares together, and display the finished quilt at your next family gathering.

Artifacts

Do you have an old watch, clothes, or anything else that belonged to any of your ancestors? If you have many such items, you could create a museum-style display to help preserve and protect them, while at the same time making them available for other family members to view and enjoy. An inexpensive display box can be made with scrap wood, leftover material, and a sheet of glass. Visit a local museum to get some ideas on how to best display your own artifacts.

Coat of Arms

Some families have a coat of arms developed in medieval times and passed down through succeeding generations. According to the ancient laws of heraldry however, few living people today are legally entitled to bear these historic symbols. Normally, the emblem must be modified by succeeding generations, if they're entitled to it at all. Rather than purchase a mail order coat of arms of dubious authenticity, why not start from scratch and create an original one for your own family? You could choose symbols to represent your family's heritage, such as a cotton boll if you're from the south. This is a chance to really give your imagination free reign. You may want to check out a book on heraldry from the library to get some ideas.

Family Flag

Countries, states, military units, and boy scout troops all have their own unique flags. Why not creat one for your own family? Fly it outside on important family dates, such as wedding anniversaries, or the day in history an ancestor arrived in America. You may also want to take it with you to family reunions, on camping trips, and to other social activities in which your family participates.

Totem Pole

Indians, eskimos, and other natives often told the stories of their families and ancestors through intricately carved poles of wood. Painted with bright colors, many still stand today as silent witness of a people and way of life almost forgotten by our fast food and throw away generation. Creating a smaller scale family history totem pole is a fun project your whole family might enjoy creating. It will also be an interesting conversation piece for all who see it.

Each section of the pole should be carved with an animal or symbol to represent something important to your family. A leprechaun's head might represent your Irish heritage; a whale might be symbolic of your forefathers' dependence on fishing for their livelihood. If your own family has traveled a lot, a bird with outstretched wings might be an appropriate representation. Make a detailed drawing of your totem pole before you start carving. After careful sanding, use bright enamel paints to finish your masterpiece. The totem pole could be planted in your front yard for all to see (beware of vandelism), or you might mount it on a base for display in your front entryway.

More, More, More!

This chapter has provided just an overview of the multitude of small projects available to the family historian. There is no limit to what you can do to help preserve your family's heritage.

If you have a hobby, more than likely there is some way you can apply it to your family history. For example, a stamp collector might create an album of stamps representing the years and places of birth for themselves and their ancestors. A coin collector could do the same thing. If you like to embroider, there is an unlimited number of wall hangings, pillows, and the like you could create.

An artist could draw or paint pictures of possible scenes from their ancestor's past. If you like acting, write a short one-act play portraying an event or scene from your family's past. If you write songs or poetry, a ballad or poem about an ancestor's life might be fun to compose.

Preserving family history should be fun. Whatever you choose to create, try to make it an enjoyable project. The reason most people fail to document their family's past is because of the mistaken belief that history is boring. It can be, as many of us learned in high school. But it doesn't have to be all dull and drudgery. Hopefully this chapter and the ones preceeding it have given you some ideas on how you might preserve your own family's heritage.

PART III
REPRODUCTION, BINDING,
& MORE

CHAPTER 20
Reproduction & Binding Methods

Books are usually somewhat of a mystery to those unfamiliar with the craft of reproduction and binding. Libraries and bookstores attest to the fact that there must be thousands of authors in America, but few people can imagine one of these books with their own name on it. To most people such a dream is only a fantasy, like riding the space shuttle or playing in the World Series.

Perhaps by now you've completed a comprehensive chronology of your family, or have compiled a who's who in family history. So what do you do with that stack of papers? Some family historians simply put them in a folder, and then move on to other things. This is a sure road to disaster! First, your priceless originals need to be reproduced, even if you want only one copy. Among the many means and methods of printing and reproduction, there are a couple that are both practical and economical for the family historian.

To protect and preserve the things you have written, the manuscripts must also be bound. Even if you want only one copy of your book, there is no reason you can't have a beautiful hard-bound edition as nice as any you've ever seen in a library. Of course, for some books you may want to use a simpler binding, such as saddle stitching, spiral, or comb binding. Whatever you choose, don't put it off until a later date. No written history is finished until it is bound. And until it is bound, there is always a chance the pages might be damaged or accidentally thrown out with other stacks of paper.

This chapter will discuss a few of the details you need to be knowledgeable about before going to visit a local printer. You should have your manuscript "camera-ready," no matter what method of printing you choose to use. We'll also discuss the two most feasible methods of reproduction for family histories, and several options you have to choose from for binding.   Check the books listed in the bibliography if you want to learn more about book production, especially if you're interested in printing a large quantity of books.

Camera-Ready Copy

The final draft of your manuscript which you take to the printer should look exactly (with the possible exception of photographs) like you want the printed and bound copy to look. This doesn't mean the pages have to be typed perfectly, however.   You can erase, cut, and paste over as much you need to, as long as you do it neatly.   You may also have the pages reduced or enlarged in printing if you desire. "Camera-ready" means only that what the camera sees is what you want the printed pages to look like - nothing more; nothing less.

Paper

There are an almost endless number of types and grades of paper used for printing.   What you choose for your family histories is largely a matter of cost and personal preference. Most papers are made from materials that have a high acid content.   As a result, the paper begins a process of disintegration almost as soon as it is created.   In less than one hundred years it may be reduced to little more than a pile of paper crumbs.   Acid-free paper is available, however it is a bit more expensive. If you want your documents to last, you should spend the extra money.

Photographs

If you're going to include photographs in your book, you have several choices for their reproduction.   The easiest and cheapest method is simple photocopying.   Tape the photographs in their desired position on your final draft, and then photocopy the pages the same way as if there were no photos. A quality copier will make surprisingly good copies from high grade prints.

If you want better quality, or especially if you are going to have your work offset printed, you will need to have halftones made from your photographs. The halftoning process changes continuous tone photographs or artwork into dots, which are then printed in the space you've designated on your manuscript pages. The photographs in this book were printed from halftones.

You've probably noticed that in many books all of the photographs are grouped together in one section of the book on higher quality paper. This keeps the cost of the book down by using lower grade paper for the majority of the book, while at the same time providing quality reproduction of the pictures. You may choose to photocopy the text of your book, have the photos halftoned and offset printed together, and then bind the two print jobs together.

The method of reproduction you choose for your photographs depends a great deal on the method of printing you're using for the rest of the book. You may want to talk to several printers and get price quotes before committing yourself to one method. They're experts at what they do, and should be able to give you valuable advice about how to proceed within the budget you've created for your project.

Printing: Photocopying

The most economical and fastest method of reproduction for a small quantity of books is photocopying. One copy of a 100-page book, at ten cents per page, would cost $10 to print. You can print the book yourself, usually at a savings, at a quick-print shop, or leave it with the printer to copy for you.

If you are copying photographs with the text by this method, be sure to find a high quality machine that will adjust to varying degrees of lightness and darkness. Experiment to see which setting gives the cleanest, clearest copy.

Most print shops charges are per copy, not per sheet. Thus, at ten cents per copy, two one-sided sheets would cost twenty cents, as would one two-sided sheet.

Offset Printing

With offset printing, a camera makes a "plate" image of a document, which is then used for printing any number of copies. This method is most economical for a large number of copies, perhaps 1000 or more. Offset printing generally gives a little bit better image than does photocopying.

Most of the expense involved in offset printing is created by the initial plate-making and set-up. Thus, the more copies you have printed, the less will be the actual cost per copy. This savings could be substantial if you are having 5,000 copies or more printed.

On the other hand, if you are only having five or ten copies printed, offset printing might be prohibitively expensive. A lot depends upon what you're printing; a 200-page book would cost thousands of dollars for even a single copy, however a two-page bio sheet might only cost one dollar each if you get one hundred or more copies printed. Of course the same bio sheet might only be twenty cents photocopied.

Hardcover Binding

I've listed hardcover binding first among binding methods because it is the most "professional," and also the most durable. Durability is of prime importance with family histories.

The easiest, and most expensive way to hardcover bind your books is to take your unbound copies to a printer, tell them what you want, and then let them take care of the rest. Such binding will cost $50-100 or more, depending upon the material used, and upon any printing you want on the cover.

For a fraction of the cost you could do the entire job yourself. Hardcovers aren't difficult to make, and binding them to your printed documents is an easy evening's work. Should you desire to go this route, your library probably has several good books giving detailed instructions on hand binding methods (see bibliography for a partial list). Or, for little more than a dollar, you can get the Boy Scouts of America merit badge booklet Bookbinding. It provides illustrated step-by-step instructions on several methods of bookbinding. Check your local scouting supply store for a copy.

Paperback Covers

Paperback book covers, like your manuscript, can be printed by either offset printing or photocopying. In addition, you may want to consider having your cover typeset by a printer to give it that "professional" look. Of course, you could accomplish the same thing yourself using pressure sensitive rub-on letters available at office supply stores. They come in all sizes and styles of type, and are easy to use. You should laminate your paperback covers with clear self-adhesive plastic sheets before you bind your book together. This will make them look even better, and will add strength and durability to what otherwise might be easily soiled and torn.

Plastic Comb Binding

The most popular type of binding for family histories is the plastic comb. Your local quick copy printer can probably bind your manuscript while you wait for only a couple dollars. Plastic combs are especially good for works such as the chronology, which needs continual updating to keep it current; pages are easily added or removed as needed, yet not so easy as to make it flimsy or fragile.

Plastic Strip Binding

Your local printer can also bind your book with a plastic strip while you wait for about the same price as the plastic comb. The strip however, is meant to permanantly bind the pages together, which will also help the book last longer than those bound with a plastic comb. Some printers also offer hardcovers that can be glued to works that are strip-bound.

Saddle & Side Stitching

Shorter works are best bound by either saddle stitching or side stitching. Many magazines are saddle stitched; they have two or three staples through the center of the pages, which are then folded over in half. If your work is offset printed, you can specify this type of binding to the printer to be done at the same time the printing is accomplished. If you're photocopying your manuscript pages, this method will only work if you want the finished "book" to be 5 1/2 X 8 1/2" or smaller. This is because the full-size sheets must be folded in half if the work is to be stapled in the middle. Most printers can saddle stitch your book for you for only a few cents per copy.

Everyone is familiar with side stitching; most pamplets that are not saddle stitched are bound with two or three staples along the left side. An ordinary stapler will do for any work less than thirty pages; anything more should probably be "stitched" with heavy duty staples.

Other Options

The methods of reproduction and binding discussed in this chapter are only the most popular and economical means available to the family historian. There are other forms of printing, such as thermography, letterpress, engraving, embossing, and foil stamping. There are also other types of binding, such as spiral, perfect, and paste. You may want to explore some of these other options for certain projects, or you may want to try to come up with something even more original.

It's been often said that "you can't judge a book by its cover." This is especially true with family history. However, a book of family history deserves the best cover and binding you can give it. The more professional and expensive your finished books look, the more likely they are to be taken care of and preserved through the ages.

CHAPTER 21
Tradition

Tradition is the hidden backbone of family history. It is the beliefs and customs that were taught to us by our parents, and those which we teach to our own children. The traditions may be either social, religious, or family oriented, and may be passed from one generation to another for many generations without our ever being aware of them. The social customs of the Middle East have endured for thousands of years with virtually no change, silently inherited by each succeeding generation.

Every family has their own unique customs and family traditions. Some customs we inherit without ever realizing they are unique to our own family; others we consciously promote and encourage because they are fun, or help build closeness and family unity. Whatever they may be, the family historian needs to be aware of these special traditions and document them in biographies, short histories, and special studies.

Be a Pioneer!

Traditions aren't limited to just the ones you learned from your own parents. They had to start someplace; why not be a pioneer in your family and start traditions that will be meaningful to you, your family, and your posterity? Two hundred years from now your descendents may say, "this tradition was started by great-great-great-great-grandpa Jones back in the twentieth century." What a legacy!

The following examples are merely a primer to get your imagination imagining. Some of these traditions teach your family about their own history; others are just plain fun and will bring your family closer together, creating fond memories for your children to reflect upon as they grow older and raise children of their own.

Christmas Traditions

The family traditions centered around the Christmas holidays are usually the most remembered and cherished. In the mind of a child, Christmas is the high point of each year – everything the family does at this time of year is accentuated. Below are some Christmas traditions others have started:

- Tree ornaments are all handmade, with at least one new ornament added each year.
- Family members go caroling together as a family; nursing homes and hospitals are favorite locations.
- Christmas cards are all handmade and decorated by parents and children as a family activity.
- Family members go sledding, skiing, or swimming (especially if you live Down Under) together on Christmas day.
- Each Christmas follows a different theme based on ancestors' homeland. One year may be a "German" Christmas, with decorations, meals, and even presents representative of the customs of Germany. The next year might be Norwegian, Irish, Mexican, or Polish, depending upon where your ancestors came from.
- Beginning right after Thanksgiving, kids like to know how many days it is until Christmas (stores have the same problem). Many families make "Christmas countdown" calendars to keep track of the days; some make a special candle with marks for each day, burning it for a few minutes each day to get it down to the next line.
- To help others and teach children the real meaning of Christmas, some families include single, widowed, and elderly friends or acquaintances in their Christmases; there are as many lonely people at Christmas as there are happy families.

Birthdays

Next to Christmas, a child's birthday is usually his second favorite day of the year. There are many ways of celebrating birthdays besides traditional cake and ice cream parties with presents.

- Sometimes families who have children with birthdays near Christmas celebrate "half-birthdays" instead.
- Whoever's birthday it is chooses a favorite meal for dinner.
- Instead of a big party with lots of children, some families invite only one family with similar age children to share in a small party or picnic or family outing.
- Annual growth is recorded permanently on a growth chart, by notches in a doorway, or by some other means.- Some couples plant a tree in the yard upon the birth of each child.
- Ancestors are remembered and honored in some families by a special dinner or activity on the anniversary of their birth.

Miscellaneous Traditions

Traditions aren't limited to things we do just once or twice each year; the ways we do some things every day may be remembered and passed down as traditions. Here is a sampling:

- One family has a special table cloth they use for guests. Each time they have visitors over for dinner, the guests sign their names on it, which is later embroidered over for a permanent record.
- Some families plan a major family outing for one Saturday each month. It needn't be something expensive, but they need to be done consistantly to be remembered as tradition.
- Many families devote one evening each week just for family activities. They may play games together, go to a movie, plan trips or vacations, or discuss important matters and concerns relevant to the family.
- Some families visit nursing homes on a regular basis to cheer up and provide companionship to the residents.- Singing is an important tradition to many families. They may sing before meals, sing in the car, or sing together before going to bed.
- Some extended families plan reunions at regular intervals. Traditionally, they may have Thanksgiving dinner at Grandma's house, or a Fourth of July picnic at Uncle Harry's mountain cabin.
- Many families have a family portrait made at the same time each year. Individual portraits may be made at the same time, or perhaps on birthdays.

147

- One family chooses the best work of art each child creates each school year, and has it professionally mounted and framed for display.

CHAPTER 22
Children & Family History

There is a reason I've chosen to conclude this book with a chapter on children and family history. In the first chapter of this book I stated that I believed the greatest reason for preserving family history was our children. They're the ones who have the most to gain from our efforts. But not only does the child benefit from reading the things that we have written, but also from recording their personal and family's history themselves.

Many of the projects which follow could have been included in other parts of this book, however I've grouped all of these together here to aid you in teaching your children the art of family history. There are side-benefits to many of these projects. Elementary school teachers have found that children show more enthusiasm and write more about subjects of which they are familiar. Many of these teachers are having their students write papers about themselves and their families. In fact, my third grader is required to keep a personal journal, in class!

You may even discover that some of the following methods will aid you in your own efforts to write. Use and adapt them to your own situation, and to the interests, talents, and abilities of your own family. Family history is a hobby that can be enjoyed by the entire family.

Interview Your Children

Oral history works well with children, especially pre-schoolers who haven't learned yet to write. After a vacation, birthday, or other fun activity, sit down with your child and a tape recorder and ask your child about what they did. You'll often get interesting and memorable comments. As the children grow older they'll ask to listen to these tapes again and again.

If you have parents or grandparents that live far away, you may want to make a taped family "letter" to send them. Ask them to keep or return the tape to you for your family archives. Or, if you have the equipment, you could make a copy of the tape before you send it.

Personal Journals

Children can begin keeping a personal journal as early as two or three years of age. In the beginning, you will have to write the entries for them. Once a week, and on important dates, ask them specific questions about what they did, and then write down their comments. The entries needn't be long; two or three sentences may suffice.

As the children learn to write, they can take over the actual writing part. In the beginning, you may have to write down their comments on a sheet of paper for them to copy into their journal. Be sure to keep it short at this stage; one or two sentences takes a long time for little hands to copy.

Set a certain day and time aside for journal writing, and stick with it. Like music lessons, journal writing will often require parental encouragement (as in "you may not want to, but one day you'll thank me for it!"). Children who develop the habit of journal-writing when they're young will probably stick with it for the rest of their life.

Story Picture Book

Children who like to draw and color could help compile a true story picture book of a family vacation, or perhaps the life of an ancestor. If they can't write yet, you or an older child could write the story while the young children provided the illustrations. A few years ago my two oldest boys and I wrote such a book, titled "The Week Before Christmas." It turned what had been several days of family conflict into a light-hearted and amusing tale. I wrote the verse, while each of the boys drew the illustrations. They were then put together in a photo album, and even today the boys love to get it down and remember the mischief they got into that year.

T'was the week before Christmas
And the boys were so bad
That Mom and Dad
Were constantly mad

Mom spent several days
Baking cookies and cake
There wasn't a thing
That she couldn't make

But the fudge we smashed
On the living room floor
And Mom said that she
Wouldn't make any more

When we knocked down the bookcase
And loudly it crashed
We thought it was over
We almost got smashed

But Mommy's nice bells
And Daddy's things too
Were broke on the floor
We didn't know what to do

My brother in bluejeans
And me in my wrap
Were put to bed early
For a long afternoon nap

But we weren't at all sleepy
And got up from the bed
And I hit my brother
With a belt on his head

T'was the week before Christmas
And the boys were so bad
That Mom and Dad
Were constantly mad

Now Christmas is over
And we're trying to be better
Santa came last night
And he left us a letter

Mom gave us presents
And so did Dad
I guess they still love us
Even when we're bad

But next Christmas is coming
Santa said in his letter
If we want him to come
We'll have to be better

There are hundreds of ways this project can be accomplished, and the pages may be bound together in a variety of fashions. Go to the public library and look at the children's books. You will come up with more ideas for children's family history books than your family could ever hope to write. Over the years you might collect shelves of such story books.

Puppet Show

Children love puppet shows. You and your children could work together to make puppets representing your ancestors. A good "stage" for such a story would be plywood with a tree painted on it, with holes cut out for each of the puppets. The story of how your family came to be could then be told on your family puppet tree. The puppet show could be presented at family gatherings, your child's school class, or at church activities.

Games & Puzzles

Many games and puzzles can be adapted to family history. You might create a "word find" puzzles that contains the names of ancestors and the countries they came from, or a game of family history trivia. In magazines I often see mail order ads for companies that will make jigsaw puzzles from photographs. Old pictures of ancestors in the form of a puzzle would help introduce your children to their forebears.

Family history lends well to travel games also. You could play a game of "Who am I?" while crossing the country on a family vacation. The person who is "it" chooses an ancestor, and then the others take turns asking questions that can be answered with a "no" or "yes." You keep playing until someone correctly identifies the ancestor. If you include aunts, uncles, and cousins, you might have quite a group to choose from. Until the children become familiar with their family members, you may have to offer clues on occassion.

Time Capsule

Children are fascinated by stories of buried treasure. Creating and burying their own treasure, complete with a treasure map, is the next best thing to finding a chest full of gold coins and precious jewels. It will also help the child visualize the link between themselves and future generations.

There are all sorts of things that can be put in a time capsule; the size of your container will dictate how much of and what items can be included. Make sure your container is air and water tight. You may even want to place the individual items in plastic bags for extra insurance. The time capsule could be for just one individual, or could be shared by the entire family. If it's to be for your whole family, you may want to have several smaller compartments or containers for individual family member's treasures. The following short list should give you some ideas of what to place in your own time capsule.

Current newspaper
Family/individual portraits
Magazine
Pictures of home, automobile
A favorite small toy
Coins and stamps in circulation/use
Recent postcard or letter from relative
An item of clothing
A piece of jewelry

Another item that could be included is a letter to the future. Your children might write a letter to their own future children, telling about themselves, their hobbies, likes, dislikes, teachers, favorite foods, favorite songs, movies, secret ambitions, etc. They could describe their family, their house, tell about pets, or relate a recent family trip or vacation. They might even want to try to predict what life will be like in the future, perhaps at the time which you've chosen for opening your time capsule.

Finally, you'll need to choose a place for burying your treasure, and decide upon a future date when it will be opened. Choose your spot carefully; property changes hands, valleys sometimes become lakes and rivers, and roads are built where none existed before. I would recommend choosing a date for digging up your time capsule at least twenty-five years in the future. Finally, don't forget to draw a detailed treasure map; you may even want to take pictures of the spot from different angles to show the relationship of the place to other landmarks. Keep these in your family archives.

Scrapbooks

Everyone is familiar with scrapbooks. They're usually oversized blank books designed for pasting brochures, ticket stubs, photographs, printed napkins, dried flowers, postcards, and all the other little odds and ends that people save from trips and other memorable occassions. Scrapbooks are often a child's first introduction to preserving their own personal history.

The format of the scrapbook also lends itself well to journals, short histories, and photograph collections. Using full-size sheets of colorful construction paper, you can glue newspaper clippings, photographs, short essays, drawings, or just about anything else that is flat to them to create scrapbook "pages." Your prepared pages can be bound in a photo album that contains plastic sleeves for 8 X 10 photographs just by slipping the page into the sleeve, and then placing them in the binder. You may want to create a separate binder for each child for each school year.

Your children will probably enjoy creating this kind of history or journal more than the kinds we adults are accustomed to. Kids like to cut, glue, and color; by combining these with short written descriptions and narratives they will create a record they'll be proud of, and one that even their own children will enjoy.

Pen Pal Letters

In addition to letters to friends and relatives, letters to pen pals will help your kids with their family history. Since pen pals have never met, they must describe themselves, their family, home, and perhaps even country to their new and distant friend. And once the relationship has been formed, regular correspondence over a period of years may be as good or better than a journal. Copies of such letters might contain a fairly complete history of one's childhood. Check with the school or library for a list of pen pal organizations.

Conclusion: A Rich Heritage

We all have an obligation to teach our children who they are, and where they came from. A child who has a strong identity will become an adult with a strong identity, a precious commodity in this age of rapid change and shallow roots.

Children love activities. The skillful teacher or parent is the one who can combine learning with an activity that is fun to do. Teaching family history is no exception. Many of us remember the boring history classes which we suffered through in high school; we must take care not to make learning or compiling family history a boring "chore." There is no reason that with a little imagination family history can't be as fun an activity as painting, playing a game, or writing a short story.

Those families in which history is important to them are more likely to create memories that will be cherished by the children and parents alike. Children have a natural curiosity about the past, and with a little direction may become skilled recorders of their own early years.

No matter what we or our parents have accomplished in this life, we are all heirs to a rich heritage. To be ignorant of this heritage is like being a "lost" heir to a million dollars, never reaping the wealth that is ours to claim.

APPENDICES

A – Sample Journal Entries

B – Sample Family Newsletter

C – Sample Document List & Documents

D – Sample Chronology

E – Sample Timetable

F – Sample Short "Bio"

G – Sample Oral History

H – Sample Pedigree Chart

I – Sample Family Group Sheet

APPENDIX A
Sample Journal Entries

5 October 1977

HUNTSVILLE, ALABAMA. This book is the beginning of what I hope
to be a lifetime journal. I will attempt to write in here at
least once a week, and more if time and thought permit. I will
try to include not only daily personal events, but also events
of national and world interest. This won't be just a book which
I only write in to relieve my daily frustrations, but a record
to myself as I grow older and to my descendents. I dedicate
this book to the most beautiful girl in the world, my wife
Joycelyn, and to our children so that they may have a better
understanding of their father. I also dedicate it to all of
those that follow these, that I may hold a special place in
their thoughts, and that they may gain some knowledge of what
will to them be history.

21 May 1978

HUNTSVILLE. Slept late this morning; I had to work last night
by myself. It was real quiet, and I didn't do much. About an
hour after coming home from church this morning Phil came over.
He told us that Rick, Dave, and Mike were in a car accident last
night. Dave and Rick were killed, and Mike was in intensive
care. It was hard to believe. I'm not looking forward to going
to work tomorrow; we were all really good friends, and there
were only eight of us that worked together. Now there will only
be five. It's going to take a lot of adjusting.

3 April 1979

LACKLAND AFB, TEXAS (Air Force Basic Training). TUESDAY. Today
was a full day. We had our hair cut this morning - all of it!
After that we got our uniforms. We also received field jackets
this morning. We were busy all day. This is the first free
minute we've had all day, and we have to be in bed by 9:00 -
about 15 minutes from now. Our drill instructors are TSgt
Miller and Sgt Barnes. So far I like Sgt Barnes the best. We
marched today, and spent quite a bit of time in class. Marching
is a lot harder than it looks. The food we've had so far is
real good, but we don't have much time to eat it.

16 April 1979

LACKLAND AFB. MONDAY. Today Joycelyn and I have been married
for two years; I could have thought of better ways to spend our
anniversary. I called her this evening, and we talked for ten
or fifteen minutes. It sure was nice. I had to sneak out of
the dorm to call her, and luckily I didn't get caught. Today
Fitzgerald got set back five days; he failed his inspection
again. Lewis got discharged today, too. He wanted to get out.

1

5 July 1979

WICHITA FALLS, TEXAS. THURSDAY. This afternoon Joycelyn and I went swimming for a little while. We both have pretty good tans now. She won't get to go too many more times this summer. I hope the baby is born within the next couple of weeks. Waiting for it is like waiting for Christmas, but not knowing which day it will come on. Could be one day, or could be another month. Basic Training seems like a long time ago. It probably won't seem too long before I'll be getting out of the Air Force. I'd like to have about four kids by then.

14 August 1979

WICHITA FALLS. TUESDAY. Today was a big day for Nathan Edward Banks. This morning Joycelyn took me to school. She was supposed to go to the hospital today for a stress test, but when she called they told her they couldn't do it today because they already had three women in labor. She went over to visit Marsha, and while she was there she started having lot stronger contractions. She called me at school at 11:20 and told me she was going to the hospital. I told her I'd meet her there after I got out at 11:50. I didn't really think it was anything, especially after yesterday. . . . At 4:25 the doctor decided to send her to delivery. He thought the baby was having too much stress. I had to change into their uniform, and when I was washing my hands one of the nurses told me I'd better hurry. I then went in and sat by Joycelyn. Finally, at 4:42 p.m., Nathan was born. He just whimpered a couple times, and then they sent him to the nursery.

25 May 1980

HUNTSVILLE, ALABAMA. SUNDAY. I haven't written since we left home over a week ago. It sure was fun surprising everyone. Everybody was really happy to see us. On the way out here, right after we got into Alabama at about 2 a.m. I fell asleep while driving. We were completely off the road when I woke up, and when I tried to get back on the road I lost control of the car and we spun around a couple times and ended up in the mud in the median. We were stuck good, and it was raining. We all went to sleep after awhile; even though we were clearly visible to both sides of the interstate and I had the flashers on, nobody stopped to help us until about 6 a.m. It was still raining, but a trucker finally got us out and on our way again.

9 December 1980

HUNTSVILLE. TUESDAY. Today is my last day at home. I leave
this afternoon at 5:15, and will be flying to Denver and then on
to San Francisco. I'm not sure yet how I'll be getting to
Travis AFB. Tomorrow night I'll fly from there to Korea. It's
going to be a long year. I sure am going to miss Nathan a lot.
I'm sure he'll forget me before long, but I think that's best.
I'd hate for him to miss me as much as I'll miss him.

3 May 1981

OSAN AB, KOREA. SUNDAY. This morning I went to the shop about
10:00, and I got a call from Job Control. They said they had a
message for me to call home. I knew then that Joycelyn must
have had the baby. I got a control number and called, but the
operator at Redstone Arsenal wouldn't put the call through. I
decided to try calling the Red Cross on the outside chance that
they might have heard something. I was lucky - they had. They
said it was a boy, 7 lbs 4 oz, 20 1/2". They didn't have a day
or time. I tried calling later, and still couldn't get
through. I finally decided to go to the Recreation Center and
call my mother collect. It was about 1 a.m. back in Alabama
when I finally got through to her. She told me that Ryan David
was born at 3:08 a.m. on the 2nd of May. That was 5:08 p.m.
yesterday my time.

21 February 1982

MADRID, SPAIN. SUNDAY. Ron Richards told me today he was going
on a trip for ten days, and asked if we would like to use his
car during that time. All I had to do was ride with him to the
airport and then take the car. He stopped in front of the main
entrance when we got there, and then he left me with the car.
After he had gone inside, I couldn't get the car to go. It
seemed to be running fine; it just wouldn't move. A Spanish
policeman who had been watching me kept yelling something to me,
but of course I couldn't understand him. Each time I put the
car in gear the tires would squeal, and then the engine would
die; for some reason the car just wouldn't move. The policeman
finally walked over and opened the passenger door, got in, and
released the parking brake. I sure was embarrassed.

19 May 1982

MADRID. WEDNESDAY. This afternoon when Joycelyn was teaching a
piano lesson Nathan came and asked me about going to the
playground, and I told him I was reading. He said "Go myself,"
and then walked out the door, waited for a car and then ran
across the street to the playground - without any pants on! I
put on my shoes, got him a pair of pants and went over to the
playground. I guess he thought it was okay to go since he had
asked me first.

3

25 December 1982

MADRID. SATURDAY (Christmas day). After playing with toys for
a while we got in the car and drove to the mountains. There was
close to a foot of snow up at Navacerrada, and we rented a
sled. There were lots of people skiing and sledding. Joycelyn
tried it first and went down the hill without knowing how to
steer or even stop the sled. There was a Spaniard just laying
on the ground at the bottom of the hill, and she hit him hard.
She didn't ride the sled any more after that.

8 November 1983

MADRID. TUESDAY. I had some things I need to do on base today,
so we left this morning to get there before noon. Right after
we left we were going around a curve out onto the highway, and
Nathan's door flew open. For several seconds he was just
hanging onto the door outside the car. I reached back and
pulled the door closed and he climbed back in. He was real
scared. Nathan said he was holding on so that he wouldn't fall
out in the road and get run over and get killed.

22 May 1985

HUNTSVILLE, ALABAMA. WEDNESDAY. This new day started where the
last one ended, with Joycelyn in the middle of labor and both of
us getting more and more tired. . . . The baby's heartbeat had
been real strong and steady throughout the whole ordeal, but
then dropped to about 60 beats per minute. The room went wild
as doctors and nurses and equipment was brought in to perform an
emergency cesarean. They made me leave then, and for the next
hour I didn't hear anything. Dr Sheppard finally came out to
talk to me. He said everything went fine and without
complication, and that Jaron Michael Banks was born at 8:25.
Nathan and Ryan are both excited about having a baby brother.
When I first talked to Ryan on the phone this morning he asked
what the baby was, and I told him it was a boy. He echoed "It's
a boy!" and I could hear Nathan say "Oh no!" from across the
room. He doesn't seem to mind any more since he got to see
Jaron though, and we're all very happy to have Jaron in our
family.

11 June 1986

WARNER ROBINS, GEORGIA. WEDNESDAY. Nathan and Ryan had their
first t-ball game this evening. Nathan was the first to bat and
got a hit, and ended up scoring the first run after getting
advanced around the bases by other hitters. Ryan got a hit and
made it to first base, but when the coach yelled for him to keep
running he ran straight to third base from first instead of
going to second. I guess he remembered watching Nathan's first
time at bat last year.

4

20 July 1986

WARNER ROBINS. WEDNESDAY. Nathan got in trouble today. Donald snuck him in his house when nobody else was home and got Nathan to make an obscene phone call. Donald told Nathan what number to call, and what to say. The lady that answered told Nathan that what he was doing was against the law, and asked him what his name was. Nathan got scared and hung up and came home crying; he thought the police were going to find out that he had made the call and they would put him in jail. He was really scared. I think he learned a good lesson from the experience.

3 February 1987

WARNER ROBINS. TUESDAY. Today was a beautiful spring day. The sky was clear most of the day, with the temperature in the upper sixties. It felt more like April than February. But the best part about today is that we now have a little baby girl! Chelsea Nicole Banks was born early this morning at 00:57 at the Robins Air Force Base hospital. . . . Nathan and Ryan were already up watching Ghost Busters on television when I woke up. I went in the living room and started watching with them, and then Jaron came in and sat down by me. Ryan asked if Mommy was at the hospital having the baby, and I told them that she already had the baby, and that they had a little sister. Nathan and Ryan were both excited about having a sister, but especially Ryan. Jaron just kept watching TV, but when I told them that Chelsea was her name, Jaron said "No!" Nathan and Ryan really thought that was funny. This afternoon we spent a couple hours decorating the front yard. We put up a banner that says "IT'S A GIRL!" and lots and lots of pink ribbons and bows on the trees in the front yard. Everyone that goes by our house will know that we finally got a girl.

30 November 1987

ANCHORAGE, ALASKA. MONDAY. It didn't snow too much last night, but it started coming down heavy a little before I left for work this morning. It's the heaviest snow I've seen yet, and it kept up for several hours. Before today Anchorage had 24 inches of snow this month - the average for November is 10 inches. Today we got at least another four or five. At 10:23, while it was still snowing fairly hard, I felt the building begin to shake. It lasted more than a minute, and felt a lot like riding a roller coaster. Pictures on the walls were rattling, and the trembling came in waves, getting stronger for a few seconds and then letting up, over and over again. The earthquake measured 7.5 on the Richter scale, and was centered 300 miles southeast of Anchorage.

APPENDIX B
Sample Family Newsletter

the Banks Family
Messenger-Journal

Number 1   SUMMER 1987   Page 1

First issue of new Family newsletter

This issue of the Banks Family Messenger-Journal marks the beginning of what we hope to be a long-time adventure into the world of newsletter publishing. Where most newsletters exist to make somebody a profit, our purpose is to create a record of our family's activities (Journal), and also to inform our distant friends and family of our daily lives and (mis?)adventures (Messenger).

We live in an age when families are often separated by thousands of miles, and when frequent reunions are impractical. Hopefully, this newsletter will help foster and maintain the communication that is so necessary to sustain relationships.

Right now we plan on an irregular publishing schedule, probably two or three times a year. This premier issue is dated "Summer 1987", and records our activities starting from the beginning of this year.

This is a family project, with Keith and Joycelyn providing most of the writing and editing, and with Nathan and Ryan helping where they are able. The children will take on greater responsibilities in producing this publication as they get older.

This premier issue has been mailed to those people for whom we have addresses. If you are reading someone else's copy, but would like to receive future issues yourself, just write and let us know. We'll add you to our mailing list.

Announcing...
Chelsea Nicole Banks

On February 3, 1987, Joycelyn gave birth to our first daughter. Weighing in at 7 lbs 11 oz, Chelsea Nicole was born early in the morning while her big brothers were all home sleeping.

Nathan, Ryan, and Jaron all got to see their baby sister later in the day, and they were all eager to hold and play with her. They also visited her the next two days, after which she and Joycelyn came home. They were welcomed with pink ribbons, bows and an "It's A Girl!" banner on the house and trees.

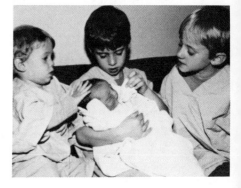

Nathan wins contest

During Easter this year Nathan and Ryan entered a coloring contest sponsored by Eckerd Drugs. They each entered two pictures, one at the Macon Mall and one at the Houston Mall.

A few days before Easter Joycelyn was notified that Nathan had won first place in his age division (7-9) at the Macon store. That evening they went to claim his prize, a hugantic easter basket filled with candy, coloring books, and a tooth brush. The winner's pictures were all displayed outside the store over the holiday.

Camping trip to Florida

On May 1-3 we took a camping trip to Florida to try out the new camping equipment we had bought in preparation for our big trip to Alaska. We had never been camping before, and this was to be a trial run before making the move in June.

All of the equipment fit in our new car-top carrier easily, with food and clothes in the trunk. The three boys sat in the back seat, with Chelsea on the floor in front of Joycelyn.

We drove down through Albany and Tallahassee, arriving at the Gulf Coast in early afternoon. Using our nifty new campground directory, we drove to a state park on St George Island.

The beaches there were nearly deserted, and there were only a few other campers in the campground. After changing clothes we drove to the nearby beach to get our first taste of salt water.

Nathan and Ryan jumped right in, playing in the waves, however Jaron said the water was "hot" (cold) and opted to play in the sand instead. Keith and Joycelyn both enjoyed swimming once they got adjusted to the cool water. Chelsea chose to just lay on the beach towel and work on her very first tan.

Jaron enjoyed pouring sand over himself so much he thought he would help Chelsea to do the same. The trip to the beach was cut short so we could go back to the showers to get the sand out of Jaron and Chelsea's hair and face.

When we returned to the campground Keith and the boys set up the tent and got their camp stove ready for dinner. We fixed cheeseburgers, hotdogs, and beans for our first meal camping out. After Jaron and Chelsea were asleep the rest of us roasted marshmellows.

After getting up the next morning a little after six, Joycelyn fixed scrambled eggs, bacon, grits, and toast for breakfast. After eating, Ryan opened his birthday presents. It was his sixth birthday, and he got several games for playing on the road.

Late in the morning we packed everything up and headed toward Panama City, looking for another campground. We found a nice one located at Tyndall Air Force Base (AFB), and chose to spend the night there. We set up the tent and unpacked the things we would be needing for our last night of camping on this trip, and then drove to Panama City Beach.

After a couple hours of swimming and playing in the sand we returned to our campsite for a dinner of grilled cheese sandwiches and frozen dinners. There were a few mosquitos at this campground, whereas the sand fleas were the trouble makers at St George.

On Sunday morning Keith fixed instant oatmeal for everyone, and then packed up some of our stuff. We then drove about fifteen miles to Mexico Beach for one last swim in the Gulf of Mexico.

The beach was beautiful, and nearly deserted. A school of dolphins swam near as Keith, Nathan and Ryan were swimming. The boys buried Keith in the sand while Chelsea tried to get a little bit more sun to add to her glowing tan.

Finally, a little before noon, we returned to Tyndall AFB to pack up the tent and leave. We drove north to Dothan, east to Albany, and then north to Warner Robins, arriving home about 9:30.

It was an enjoyable and trouble-free trip. The weather was perfect, and the kids were all well-behaved. And most importantly, it prepared us for our big trip to Alaska, barely a month away.

APPENDIX C
Sample Document List and Documents

Banks Family

Documents

Temple Sealing Certificate

This Certifies that

Keith Edward Banks _and_ Joycelyn Gay Foster

of Madison, Alabama

who were previously legally married on the Sixteenth day of April _19_ 77

at Huntsville, Alabama . were **Sealed** by me as husband
and wife according to the Ordinance of God for Time and for all Eternity, in the
Washington Temple at Kensington, Maryland, on the Ninth day of August
in the year of Our Lord One Thousand Nine Hundred and Seventy-Eight .

In the presence of

William H. Jammer _Witness_

David M. Jammer _Witness_

An Elder of the Church of Jesus Christ of Latter-day Saints

Volume VIII

DOCUMENT LIST

0001   Birth Certificate, Chelsea Nicole Banks, 3 Feb 1987, State of Georgia, File 110-87-004760.

0002   Graduation Program (Keith Banks), Seoul American High School, Seoul Korea, June 1975.

0003   Pay Stubs, Newsom Music Center to Keith Banks, 13 Nov 76 through 21 Dec 76.

0004   Form 1040A (U.S. Individual Income Tax Return), 1978, Keith and Joycelyn Banks.

0005   College Transcript, Keith Banks, Austin Community College, 27 Jan 81.

0006   Letter, Edward Weldon, Director of Georgia Department of Archives and History to Keith Banks, concerning book Wellston Air Depot: A Media View, 1941-1943, 23 Feb 87.

0007   Report Card, Keith Banks, Balboa Kindergarten, Spokane, Washington, 23 May 63.

0008   Newspaper Article, "Kingston News," The Cherry Hill News, 21 Jul 66, reporting championship of Keith Banks' little league baseball team.

0009   Marriage Certificate, Keith Banks and Joycelyn Foster, 16 Apr 77.

0010   Last Will and Testament, Keith E. Banks, 15 Apr 81.

0011   Form W-2, 1979, U.S. Air Force to Keith Banks

0012   Bank Statement, Pentagon Federal Credit Union to Keith Banks, 31 Dec 86.

0013   Loan Agreement, Bergstrom Federal Credit Union to Keith Banks, 19 Jul 1985, for $1500 loan.

0014   Receipt for Wedding Rings, Mason Jewelers, Huntsville, Alabama, 9 Oct 1976.

0015   Alabama Driver's License, Keith E. Banks, issued Jan 1985.

0016   Performance Schedule, Sino-American Dragon Dance Team Activities in Chinese Lunar New Year, 1979, with Keith Banks, and others, participating.

1

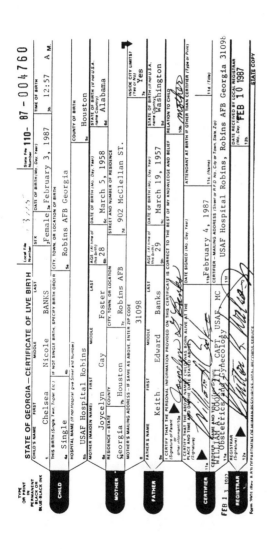

0001

STATE OF GEORGIA — CERTIFICATE OF LIVE BIRTH

TYPE OR PRINT IN PERMANENT BLACK OR BLUE-BLACK INK

State File Number 110- 87 - 004760

Local File Number

CHILD

1 CHILD'S NAME — FIRST: Chelsea MIDDLE: Nicole LAST: BANKS

2 SEX: Female 3a DATE OF BIRTH (Mo. Day, Year): February 3, 1987 3b TIME OF BIRTH: 12:57 A.M.

4a THIS BIRTH (Single, Twin, Triplet, Etc.): Single 4b IF NOT SINGLE BIRTH, SPECIFY BIRTH ORDER

5a CITY, TOWN OR LOCATION OF BIRTH: Robins AFB Georgia 5c COUNTY OF BIRTH: Houston

5b HOSPITAL NAME (If not hospital, give Street and Number): USAF Hospital Robins

MOTHER

6a MOTHER (MAIDEN NAME) — FIRST: Joycelyn MIDDLE: Gay LAST: Foster

6b AGE (At time of this birth): 28 6c DATE OF BIRTH (Mo. Day, Year): March 5, 1958 6d STATE OF BIRTH (If not U.S.A. name Country): Alabama

7a RESIDENCE—STATE: Georgia 7b COUNTY: Houston 7c CITY, TOWN OR LOCATION: Robins AFB

7d STREET AND NUMBER OF RESIDENCE: 902 McClellan ST.

7e MOTHER'S MAILING ADDRESS—IF SAME AS ABOVE, ENTER ZIP CODE: 31098

7f INSIDE CITY LIMITS? (Yes or No): Yes

FATHER

8 FATHER'S NAME — FIRST: Keith MIDDLE: Edward LAST: Banks

9a AGE (At time of this birth): 29 9b DATE OF BIRTH (Mo. Day, Year): March 19, 1957 9d STATE OF BIRTH (If not U.S.A. name Country): Washington

CERTIFIER

9e I CERTIFY THAT THE PERSONAL INFORMATION PROVIDED ON THIS CERTIFICATE IS CORRECT TO THE BEST OF MY KNOWLEDGE AND BELIEF

(Signature of Parent or other informant): [signature]

10a I CERTIFY THAT THE ABOVE NAMED CHILD WAS BORN ALIVE AT THE PLACE AND TIME AND ON THE DATE STATED ABOVE (Signature): [signature]

10b RELATION TO CHILD: Mother

10c ATTENDANT AT BIRTH IF OTHER THAN CERTIFIER (Type or Print)

11a CERTIFIER — NAME AND TITLE (Type or Print): WILLIAM A. COOK III, CAPT USAF MC Obstetrics and Gynecology

11b DATE SIGNED (Mo. Day, Year): February 4, 1987

11c (Name)

11d CERTIFIER — MAILING ADDRESS (Street or RFD No. City or Town, State, Zip): USAF Hospital Robins, Robins AFB Georgia 31098

11e (Title)

REGISTRAR

12a REGISTRAR (Signature): [signature]

12b DATE RECEIVED BY LOCAL REGISTRAR (Mo. Day, Year): FEB 10 1987

FEB 1 3 1987

Form 3401 (Rev. R.R.9) DEPARTMENT OF HUMAN RESOURCES-VITAL RECORDS SERVICE

STATE COPY

This is to certify that this is a true and correct copy of the certificate filed with the Vital Records Service, Georgia Department of Human Resources. This certified copy is issued under the authority of Chapter 31-10, Vital Records Code of Georgia.

[signature] Michael R. Jowin
State Vital Records Registrar and Custodian. Director, Vital Records Service

County Custodian [signature] Clinton X Watson Jr

Issued by [signature] MDC

Date: 5-11-87

(Void without original signature and impressed seal.)

PROGRAM

Prelude	
Processional "Pomp and Circumstance"	Sir Edward Elgar
US National Anthem	Francis Scott Key
Invocation	Cha plain R. W. Kohl
Welcome	Debra Grim
Introduction of Speaker	Thomas Drohan
Graduation Address	Richard H. Dickie
SCA Scgolars hips	Lt. Col. Lillian Martin
Original Song	Keith Banks Christi Brown
Presentation of Flowers	Michele Littlejohn Cynthia Desrochers
Valedictory	Susan Grasser
Presentation of Class	Miss Arline Didier
Presentation of Diplomas	Mr. Clarence Hinch Miss June Mitchell
Presentation of Senior Flag	Thomas Drohan
Class Ceremony	Thomas Drohan
Congratulation	Willington L. Mock
Benediction	Father Anthony Gagliardo

Pianist - Miss Lou Ann Skinner

CLASS OFFICERS

President	Thomas Drohan
Vice President	Debra Grim
Secretary	Cynthia Desrochers
Treasurer	Michele Littlejohn

LIST OF HONORS

Valedictorian	Susan Graesser
Salutatorian	Debra Grim

0002

+* Ahn, Natalie
Allen, Desiree
Allor, Jane
Anderson, Mary Ann
Andre, Denise
Atkins, Marshall
Bailey, Charlene
+* Bakarich, Tara Ashley
Bandarrae, Frederick
Banks, Keith
Behger, Mike
Bezio, James
Brewer, Jo Maureen
Brown, Sheila
Bryson, Cynthia
Buell, Karen
Cantrell, Reynolds
+ Carmichael, Therese
Carrigan, Marion
+* Christiansen, Dale
Colaianni, Mary
Cole, Deborah
Coo, Michael
Corder, Rebecca
Cromartie, Michael
Cromartie, Valorie
+ Davis, Michael
+ Davis, Steven
Demps, Billy
* Desrochers, Cynthia
Deitchman, Debra
Diaz, Robert
Dinger, Michael
+* Drohan, Thomas
Dudley, Gloria
+* Duvick, Sue

Flanagan, Kathleen
Flanagan, Patricia
Fogel, Candace
French, William
Garneav, Denise
Gascon, Robert
Gates, Sandra
Gonzales, Frank
+* Graesser, Susan
+* Grim, Debra
Grimes, Kenneth
+* Harrington, Kathy
Hathorn, George Kevin
Haughery, Anne
Hayes, Ronald
Hayes, Terry
Hirsch, George
Hollingsworth, Ronald
* Howe, Frances
Howell, Sandi
Hunt, Patricia
* Huston, Kip
Jamison, Earl Michael
Lane, Celeste
+* Lee, Sung Hee
Lehmann, Christine
Lehmann, Thomas
* Leonard, Barbara
Light, Steven
Litka, Calvin
Littlejohn, Mark
Littlejohn, Michele
McElroy, Un Kyong
McGarity, Patricia
McReynolds, Roger

Mahoney, Daniel
* Martinez, Anastasia V.
+* Merola, Wendy
Miller, Dana
Mozey, David
Murphy, John
Musick, Renee
Musick, Timothy
Nahar, Safril
Olenik, Judith
Parrot, Linda
Porter, David
Robinson, Maurice
Rose, Billy
+* Rowan, Madeline
Ruff, Giselle
Schreiber, James
Schubert, Wayne
Serrato, Rocco
Sokol, Heide
Southworth, Andre
Striker, Ted
Twilley, Lisa
Ventrice, Barbara
Vince, Victoria
+ Vinson, Veronica
Washington, Lester
+* Watson, John Mark
Webb, Alicia
Weimar, Grace
Whittengurg, Connie
Wolfe, Barbara

* National Honor Society

+ The Society of Distinguished American High School Students

0005

AUSTIN COMMUNITY COLLEGE SYSTEM
P O BOX 2165
AUSTIN, TEXAS 78767
FICE CODE 012015
STUDENT RECORD

FORM NO 8-91

SOCIAL SECURITY NO.

STUDENT NAME: BANKS KEITH E
STREET & NUMBER: PSC BOX 2093/APO
CITY STATE ZIP CODE: SAN FRANCIS CA 96366

HIGH SCHOOL / LOCATION / DATE GRADUATED

FICE CODE 001055

LAST COLLEGE ATTENDED / LOCATION

DATE PRINTED 01/27/81 — MAJOR 4301 GENERAL STUDIES
MODE OF ADMISSION: TRANSFER — ADMISSION STATUS: GOOD STANDING — ENTRY DATE 01/80
BIRTHDATE 03/19/57 — BIRTHPLACE SPI.KA — SEX M

DEGREES AWARDED: ASSOC ARTS — DATE 01/80
****
IN DIST
****

PROGRAM	COURSE NUMBER	COURSE TITLE	CONTACT HOURS LECTURE	CONTACT HOURS LAB	SEM CREDIT HOURS	G R A D E	PREV SEM HOURS	GRADE POINTS
		NON-TRADITIONAL CREDIT						
ECO	1623	SURV ECO II			3.0	CR		
ENG	1613	ENG COMP II			3.0	CR		
PSY	1613	INTRO TO PSY			3.0	CR		
PSY	1643	CHILD GRO DEV			3.0	CR		
SOC	1613	INTRO SOC			3.0	CR		
		******************						
		SPRING 1979-80						
ECO	1633	P311 MACRO ECO			3.0	A	12	
GOV	2613	US GOVERNMENT I			3.0	A	9	
		CURRENT ATT. FOR GPA EARN GPA						
		TC DATE: 6 6 21 3.500						
		GOOD SCHOLASTIC STANDING 24 3.500						
		****************** SUMMER 1979-80 ******************						
GOV	2623	TX GOV SLF-PAC			3.0	B	9	
HIS	1613	US HISTORY I			3.0	C	6	
HIS	1623	US HISTORY II			3.0	C	6	
		CURRENT ATT. FOR GPA EARN GPA						
		TC DATE: 9 9 21 2.333						
		GOOD SCHOLASTIC STANDING 15 33 42 2.300						
		END OF RECORD						

Clifton Van Dyke
DIRECTOR OF ADMISSIONS & RECORDS

OFFICIAL COPY

Secretary of State
Department of Archives and History
330 Capitol Avenue S.E.
Atlanta, Georgia 30334

Max Cleland
SECRETARY OF STATE
(404) 656-2881

Edward Weldon
DIRECTOR
(404) 656-2358
INFORMATION (404) 656-2393

February 23, 1987

Mr. Keith E. Banks
Office of History
Warner Robins Air Logistics Center
Robins Air Force Base, Georgia 31098

Dear Mr. Banks:

Thank you very much for the donation of your recent book <u>Wellston</u> <u>Air</u>
<u>Depot: A</u> <u>Media</u> <u>View, 1941-1943</u>. We are very pleased to add this volume to
our collection. Publications of this type are a valuable asset to the
research offerings provided by the Georgia Department of Archives and
History. Your efforts in compiling this book are appreciated, and I assure
you that the information you provide will be invaluable to our researchers
and staff.

We appreciate your interest in the history of our state. Again, thank you
for your donation.

Sincerely yours,

Edward Weldon

Edward Weldon

EW/mba

cc: Secretary of State Max Cleland

APPENDIX D
Sample Chronology

1957

1958

Banks Family
History

1977

1979

Chronology

1981

1985

1987

CHRONOLOGY

10 May 1956	Edward W. Banks and Bessie F. Grider married in Huntsville, Alabama.
19 Mar 1957	Keith Edward Banks born at Sacred Heart Hospital in Spokane, Washington, to Edward and Bessie Banks. Family lived at 708 W. Cleveland, Spokane, Washington.
5 Mar 1958	Joycelyn Gay Foster born at Huntsville Hospital in Huntsville, Alabama, to William (Jack) Foster and Frances Foster. Joycelyn lived at 813 Capshaw Rd in Madison, Alabama, with her mother and grandparents.
6 Mar 1959	Keith awarded "Honorable Mention" in the Baby Spokane contest.
19 Mar 1961	Keith had measles on fourth birthday - no party.
Feb 1962	Keith on Romper Room for two weeks (KREM TV, Channel 2, Spokane)
30 Apr 1963	Roger Dale Banks born in Spokane to Bessie and Edward Banks. Family lived at 6510 N. Belt.
31 Oct 1963	On Halloween, Keith appeared in costume on page 17 of the Spokane Daily Chronicle.
May 1964	Keith in the hospital for six days with pneumonia.
May 1965	Keith started playing little league baseball. He knocked in the winning run his first time at bat.
Feb 1966	Banks family moved to Cherry Hill, New Jersey. Had to give Keith's dog Misty away before leaving Spokane.
Jan 1967	Banks family moved to El Paso, Texas.
Jun 1968	Banks family moved to Mundelein, Illinois.
18 Oct 1968	Keith went hunting for the first time with his father and cousin Danny Wicklund, near Big Falls, Minnesota. Keith killed a squirrel and a partridge.

May 1969	Keith's first date, with Julia Albach and her parents.
Jul 1969	Banks family moved to Pirmasens, West Germany. Neil Armstrong stepped onto the moon the night before they left the United States.
Jul 1970	Banks family moved to Huntsville, Alabama.
Sep 1970	Keith began bowling in Jive Five league.
Sep 1972	Banks family made cross-country trip by car while moving from Alabama to Seoul, South Korea.
Oct 1972	Keith began taking Tae Kwon Do lessons.
Jun-Aug 1973	Keith's first job, working as summer hire in Civilian Pay Office on Yongsan Army Post.
Jul 1973	Keith awarded 1st Degree Black Belt in Tae Kwon Do.
4 Aug 1973	Keith attempted to break the world's endurance record for yo-yoing. Feat was attempted in the studios of AFKN TV and Radio. Was also publicized in the Pacific Stars & Stripes. He yo-yoed non-stop for 9 hours and 10 minutes, but later found out that it didn't break the record.
Jun-Aug 1974	Keith worked as summer hire in the South Post Chapel as a chaplain's assistant to a Protestant and a Jewish chaplain.
Feb 1975	Keith had new girlfriend - Cristi Brown.
24 May 1975	Keith baptized a member of the Church of Jesus Christ of Latter-day Saints by Elder Robert Barrardi.
4 Jun 1975	Keith graduated from Seoul American High School. Sang "My New Life Starts Today" with Cristi.
Jun-Jul 1975	Keith worked as summer hire in the Civilian Personnel Office.
Jul 1975	Banks family moved to Huntsville, Alabama.
Sep 1975	Keith received "Dear John" letter from Cristi.
Dec 1975	Keith started college at the University of Alabama in Huntsville as a music major.

14 Mar 1976	Keith met Joycelyn Foster at church.
16 Apr 1976	Keith and Joycelyn's first date. Went to Passion Play at local church, then up on mountain to view city lights.
30 Aug 1976	Joycelyn went away to Judson College, two hundred miles south of Huntsville.
11 Sep 1976	Keith began work as part-time sales person at Newsom Music Center in The Mall.
29 Nov 1976	Keith promoted to Assistant Manager of Newsom Music Center.
15 Dec 1976	Joycelyn home from school for the Christmas holidays. Keith gave Joycelyn an engagement ring; she didn't return to school in January.
Feb 1977	Keith quit work at Newsom's and started Banks Vinyl Service, doing vinyl repair for restaurants and auto dealers.
16 Apr 1977	Keith Banks and Joycelyn Foster married at Mount Zion Baptist Church by Reverand Joe Anglin.
16-29 Apr 1977	Keith and Joycelyn honeymoon in Florida. They traveled down the Atlantic coast, out to Key West, back through the Everglades and up the Gulf Coast before returning to their home at West Valley trailer park in Madison, Alabama.
24 May 1977	Keith and Joycelyn started working 3d shift at GTE Automatic Electric making telephones.
Apr 1978	Keith and Rick Schulz start part-time business, Signs of the Time Advertising.
21 May 1978	Three of Keith's co-workers in car accident. Rick Schulz and Dave McMahan were killed, and Mike Thigpen was seriously injured.
6 Jul 1978	Joycelyn found out that she had miscarried.
9 Aug 1978	Keith and Joycelyn sealed in the Washington Temple of the Church of Jesus Christ of Latter-day Saints.
25 Sep 1978	Keith sworn into the Air Force Inactive Reserve in the Delayed Enlistment Program. Will enter active duty 2 April 1979.

3 Nov 1978	Keith and Joycelyn quit jobs at Automatic Electric.
12 Dec 1978	Keith and Joycelyn left Huntsville for Taipei, Taiwan to visit with Keith's family for several months.
16 Dec 1978	President Carter announced decision to break formal relations with Taiwan, and establish diplomatic relations with Communist China. Resulted in several weeks of protests and demonstrations in Taipei. Americans were advised to stay off the streets.
Jan-Feb 1979	Keith performed with the Sino-American Dragon Dance Team during the Chinese New Year celebrations.
16 Mar 1979	Keith and Joycelyn returned to Huntsville.
2 Apr 1979	Joycelyn and her mother drove Keith to Nashville where he was sworn into the United States Air Force (six-year enlistment) with the rank of Airman Basic. He flew to Lackland Air Force Base, Texas, arriving late evening. This was Keith and Joycelyn's first night apart in almost two years of marriage.
16 May 1979	Keith graduated from Air Force Basic Training, and traveled to Sheppard AFB (Wichita Falls, Texas).
24 May 1979	Keith began more than three months of training in the Telecommunications Equipment Maintenance Specialist technical school.
28 May 1979	Joycelyn joined Keith at their new home in Wichita Falls.
13 Jul 1979	Keith had to have his wedding band cut off because he would be working on electrical equipment. It was the first time it had been off since Joycelyn put it on his finger at their wedding.
14 Aug 1979	Nathan Edward Banks born to Keith and Joycelyn Banks at 4:42 p.m. at Sheppard AFB Hospital.
18 Sep 1979	After graduating from tech school, Keith, Joycelyn and Nathan moved to Austin, Texas. Keith's first duty assignment was the 12th Tactical Intelligence Squadron at Bergstrom AFB.

14 Jan 1980	Keith started two college classes at Austin Community College.
28 Apr 1980	Saw President Carter at Wilford Hall, San Antonio, while taking Nathan to see doctor.
8 May 1980	Nathan had minor surgery at Wilford Hall to open blocked tear duct.
late Jun 1980	Nathan took first steps alone.
14 Aug 1980	Keith awarded an Associate of Arts Degree from Austin Community College.
2 Sep 1980	Keith got bit by snake on ankle at rest stop along the side of the road. Caused severe pain and swelling for about a week, but no illness.
9 Dec 1980	Keith left Joycelyn and Nathan in Huntsville while he spent a year on remote assignment at Osan Air Base, Korea.
4 Jan 1981	Keith cut off the end of his thumb using paper cutter in a photography darkroom (it eventually grew back).
2 May 1981	Ryan David Banks born to Keith and Joycelyn Banks at 3:08 a.m. at Limestone County Hospital in Athens, Alabama. Keith found out about it the next day.
20 May 1981	Keith began wearing glasses.
1 Jun 1981	Keith appointed to Non-commissioned Officer (NCO) status, with the rank of Sergeant.
30 Jul-20 Aug	Keith took leave and returned to Huntsville. Saw Ryan for the first time.
6 Dec 1981	Keith left Korea and spent Christmas holidays in Huntsville before moving the family to Spain.
7 Jan 1982	Keith, Joycelyn, and boys moved to Madrid, Spain.
5 Mar 1982	Ryan took first steps alone.
9 Jul 1982	Keith got to see and take pictures of Jack Nicklaus and Steve Ballesteros play eighteen holes of golf at the golf course in Moraleja, just a couple miles from home.

22 Jan 1983	Keith played "Love'n You, Forever" in the base level Air Force Talent Contest, winning first place.
23-28 Jan 1983	Joycelyn in the hospital for surgery on her jaw. Jaw was wired shut until 27 April.
13 Jun 1983	Ryan fell off bed, breaking collar bone.
14 Jun 1983	Keith signed publishing contract with Heritage Books, Inc for writing how-to book about writing family history.
27 Oct 1983	Keith found out that his photograph "Harmony" won second place in the USAFE photography contest.
1 Nov 1983	Keith appointed Squadron Historian as an additional duty. Job required writing a quarterly history of squadron activities and operations.
27 Nov 1983	Keith took pictures of a 747 that crashed near Madrid, killing more than 180 passengers.
27-31 Dec 1983	Joycelyn went on a tour to Paris; was a Christmas present from Keith.
19 Feb 1984	Keith took pictures of a large anti-NATO march from Madrid to Torrejon.
7-14 Apr 1984	Keith averaged 188 in the Mediterranean Regional Bowling Championships at San Vito AB, Italy, finishing in 2nd place.
15-20 Apr 1984	Keith bowled in the USAFE Bowling Championship at Bitburg AB, Germany.
28 Apr 1984	Keith was chosen to be one of 18 "VIPs" to christen the lanes of the new bowling alley at Torrejon AB. He got a strike on the first ball to be rolled on lane 17.
22 May 1984	Joycelyn found out that she had miscarried.
15 Aug 1984	Keith bowled his highest game to date, a 270.
17 Sep 1984	Joycelyn took Nathan and Ryan to auditions for Christmas toy commercials. Neither one was selected.

11 Jan 1985	Keith, Joycelyn, and boys left Spain. Keith went to Robins AFB, Georgia to spend his last few months in the Air Force. The rest of the family moved into a house in New Market, Alabama.
9 May 1985	Keith out-processed from the Air Force, and moved to New Market (near Huntsville) with family.
22 May 1985	Jaron Michael Banks born to Keith and Joycelyn Banks by emergency cesarean at Huntsville Hospital.
2 Jul 1985	Keith reenlisted in the Air Force for four years at Robins AFB, Georgia.
6 Jul 1985	Joycelyn and boys moved to Warner Robins, Georgia with Keith.
15 Aug 1985	Nathan rode his new bicycle without training wheels.
16 Aug 1985	Keith and Joycelyn started part-time business, The Rentlist. It was a weekly listing of local houses, trailers, and apartments for rent. Failed after only one month.
26 Nov 1985	Joycelyn went to work part-time for Sears in the Macon Mall selling sewing machines and vacuum cleaners.
30 Dec 1985	After their car broke down, Nathan rode Keith on his bicycle part way to car dealer so Keith could pick up their new car, a 1986 Buick Somerset.
1 Jan 1986	Keith, Joycelyn, Nathan and Ryan saw Halley's Comet while visiting in Huntsville.
28 Jan 1986	Space shuttle Challenger exploded while Keith was on an exercise at Ft Bragg, North Carolina.
3 Mar 1986	Keith began work as a full-time Air Force historian; was assigned to the Warner Robins Air Logistics Center History Office.
15 Mar 1986	Joycelyn had wreck in new car while on the way to work in Macon. No one was hurt, and damage to the car was minor.

1 May 1986	Keith and Joycelyn bought their first color television.
Jun 1986	Ryan learned to swim before Nathan, and was jumping off the high dive before the end of the month.
23 Aug 1986	Joycelyn attended high school 10-year reunion dinner and dance; received award for the "Most Children" with 3 1/2.
27 Aug 1986	Keith began six-month intensive effort to locate other graduates of overseas schools. Articles about his search were published in newspapers around the world, however he had few responses.
3 Feb 1987	Chelsea Nicole Banks born to Keith and Joycelyn Banks at 12:57 a.m. at Robins AFB Hospital, Georgia.
5 Feb 1987	Keith interviewed by reporter from the Macon Telegraph & News for article about book Keith compiled concerning the beginnings of Robins AFB, and also about his work with his own family history. Article and photograph appeared in 13 February newspaper.
25 Feb 1987	Keith attended the first meeting of the Macon Telegraph & News Editorial Pages Advisory Board, of which he was a member.
Jun 1987	Banks family traveled more than 7,800 miles across the United States and Canada by car during move to Anchorage, Alaska.
5 Sep 1987	Keith baptized Nathan a member of the Church of Jesus Christ of Latter-day Saints.
Sep 1987	Nathan became a Cub Scout, while Joycelyn became a Cub Scout den leader.
11-22 Nov 1987	Keith returned to Alabama for the Worldwide Air Force Historian's Workshop at Maxwell AFB.
17 Mar 1988	Keith sent book manuscript to Heritage Books, Inc., asking if they were still interested in publishing the book they agreed to publish back in 1983. (The rest is history)

APPENDIX E
Sample Timetable

BANKS FAMILY HISTORY

	World	America	
1977	Menachem Begin of Israel and Anwar Sadat of Egypt meet in Israel and Egypt to discuss peace. Leonid Brezhnev becomes president of USSR. "Punk Rock" gains popularity in Great Britain. Earthquake in Rumania kills 1,541. Cyclone in India kills 20,000, leaving more than 2 million homeless. Two 747s collide on the runway in the Canary Islands, killing 582 passengers.	Most draft-evaders from Vietnam War pardoned by President Carter. Movie Saturday Night Fever popular, starting the "Disco Dancing" craze. Movie Star Wars ushers in new era of high tech special effects movies. Spacecrafts Voyager 1 and Voyager 2 launched on journey to Jupiter and Saturn. Gary Gilmore was first person to be executed in the United States in ten years.	
1978	Violent riots break out in Iran against the Shah. Red Brigades kidnap and murder former premier of Italy. Sandinistas of Nicaragua fight against the Somoza regime. Soviet nuclear satellite crashes in remote area of Canada. Scientists study the Shroud of Turin. Soviet cosmonauts spend 96 days in space aboard space station.	U.S. establishes full diplomatic relations with Communist China. New Panama Canal treaty ratified by U.S. Senate. Mideast peace talks held at Camp David with Presidents Carter, Sadat, and Begin. California voters approve Proposition 13, cutting property taxes. 911 members of the Peoples Temple die in mass murder-suicide at Jonestown, Guyana.	

TIMETABLES

Local	Banks Family	
Southern Airlines flight 242 crashes enroute from Huntsville to Atlanta, killing 12 Huntsvillians.

Constitution Hall Park completed in downtown Huntsville.

In its first full season, Alabama A&M University soccer team places first in NCAA Division II.

Space shuttle Enterprise arrives in Huntsville for testing.

Madison County one of only three counties in the nation to establish numbering for houses outside of city limits. | Keith quit job at Newsom Music Center, and began Banks Vinyl Service.

Keith and Joycelyn sang in choral production of "The Creation" at the Von Braun Civic Center in Huntsville.

Keith Banks and Joycelyn Foster married at Mt Zion Baptist Church, Madison, Alabama.

Keith and Joycelyn began working at GTE Automatic Electric.

Ed, Bessie, and Roger Banks move back to Korea.

Keith and Joycelyn began doing genealogy research. | **1977** |
| KKK and black demonstrators exchange gunfire in downtown Decatur.

"Southwest Molester" terrorizes southwest Huntsville and surrounding areas.

DDT found in river near Triana - residents have been eating contaminated fish for 30 years.

Sherrif Headrich of Huntsville sent to prison for civil rights violations and for accepting gambling bribes. | John Wilcox hospitalized for heart attack.

Ed, Bessie, and Roger Banks move from Korea to Taipei Taiwan."

Keith and Joycelyn sealed in Washington Temple, visit Philadelphia, New York City.

Keith sworn into the Air Force Reserve, to enter active duty in April 1979.

Keith and Joycelyn visit relatives in northern Minnesota.

Keith and Joycelyn fly to Taiwan to visit Keith's family for three months. | **1978** |

APPENDIX F
Sample Short "Bio"

Biography

Keith Edward Banks

Keith Banks was born March 19, 1957 in Spokane, Washington. His mother, Bessie F. Grider, was originally from Hollywood, Alabama. His father, Edward W. Banks was born in Minneapolis, Minnesota. Keith's only brother, Roger, was born April 30, 1963 in Spokane.

Keith made his television debut when only four years of age on the locally produced Romper Room show. He took figure skating lesson for two years while living in Spokane, and when in the third grade at Balboa Elementary he also took violin lessons for a short time.

Ed Banks spent his entire career working for the Department of Defense, and beginning in 1965 was required to make frequent moves to different locations around the world. In February 1965 the family moved to Cherry Hill, New Jersey.

While living in Cherry Hill Keith became a Cub Scout. It was to be his only experience in scouting until becoming an Assistant Scout Master in 1987.

In January 1966 the Banks family moved to El Paso, Texas. Keith continued to play little league baseball, which he had started the year before leaving Spokane. The family also took up rock collecting as a hobby.

In June 1968 Keith's family moved to Mundelein, Illinois. During the sixth grade he "discovered" girls, and had his first date with a classmate, Julia Albach. He also retired from baseball after the 1969 season.

While Neil Armstrong was making his history-making trip to the moon in July 1969, the Banks' were making their own trip abroad. They moved to Pirmasens, West Germany, and during their year in Europe visited France, Italy, Switzerland, Austria, Belgium, The Netherlands, and Great Britain.

In July 1970 the Banks family moved to Huntsville, Alabama. During his two years there, Keith bowled in a junior bowling league, and averaged about 135.

During September 1972 Keith and his family travelled across the United States while making a move to Seoul, South Korea. On their way they visited friends in Spokane for the first time since leaving in 1965.

Keith's first job, at the age of 16, was managing the payroll for about 200 other summer hires in the Yongsan Army Post Civilian Pay Office. The next summer he worked as a Chaplain's Assistant, and the summer after that he worked in the Civilian Personnel Office. He graduated from Seoul American High School in June 1975.

Keith had several steady girlfriends while living in Korea. Cristi Brown, the last one, helped to convert Keith to her faith, and in May 1975 Keith was baptized a member of the Church of Jesus Christ of Latter-day Saints.

During his three years in Korea, Keith learned to play the guitar and organ. He took up photography as a hobby, and also wrote numerous songs. During his senior year of high school he played parts in four different school and community theater productions. He also served one year as president of his bowling league.

In July 1975 the Banks family moved back to Huntsville, Alabama. Keith worked for a short time as a salesman for the Consumer Service Club before entering the University of Alabama in Huntsville in December as a music major.

Keith met Joycelyn Foster at church in March 1976, and they began dating in April. Joycelyn went away to college at the end of summer, but made frequent weekend trips home throughout the fall. In September Keith began working for Newsom Music Center part-time, and was promoted to Assistant Manager in November.

After only one semester of their shuttle relationship, Keith and Joycelyn decided to get married. Joycelyn quit school, and shortly after that Keith quit his job. He became self-employed, starting Banks Vinyl Service.

On April 16, 1977 Keith and Joycelyn were married at Mt Zion Baptist Church, the church Joycelyn had attended as a child. After honeymooning for two weeks in Florida, they moved into West Valley trailer park in Madison, Alabama.

Keith gave up his business in May, and he and Joycelyn both found jobs building telephones at GTE Automatic Electric. They worked third shift for about six months before spending another year working second shift.

In August 1978 Keith and Joycelyn were sealed in the Washington Temple of the Church of Jesus Christ of Latter-day Saints. During their time off from work they also began doing genealogy research into their families' past.

In September Keith decided to join the Air Force, and was sworn into the Inactive Reserve. Since he wouldn't be going to basic training until April 1979, Keith and Joycelyn decided to visit with Keith's parents, who were now living in Taiwan. They quit their jobs in November, and made the trip to Taipei shortly before Christmas.

While in Taiwan Keith performed with the Sino-American Dragon Dance Team during the Chinese New Year celebrations. Joycelyn was also pregnant during this time.

Keith and Joycelyn returned to Huntsville in March, and on April 2, 1979 Keith enlisted for six years in the U.S. Air Force. He spent six weeks in basic training at Lackland AFB, Texas, and then went to Sheppard AFB at Wichita Falls, Texas for three and a half months of training to be a telecommunications maintenance specialist.

Joycelyn joined Keith in Wichita Falls shortly after his arrival in May, and on August 14th their first child, Nathan Edward, was born.

In September Keith graduated from tech school, and they moved to Austin, Texas. Keith was assigned to the 12th Tactical Intelligence Squadron at Bergstrom Air Force Base. During his tour there he took classes at Austin Community College, and was awarded an Associate of Arts Degree in August 1980.

In December 1980 Keith was reassigned to the 2146th Communications Group at Osan Air Base, Korea. Since it was an unaccompanied assignment, Joycelyn and Nathan returned to Huntsville for their forced year-long separation. Joycelyn was four months pregnant when Keith left.

On May 2, 1981 Ryan David was born in Athens, Alabama; Keith found out about his birth the next day. Keith didn't get to see Ryan until August, when he took a month's leave and returned to Alabama.

Keith left Korea in early December, and shortly after Christmas he moved Joycelyn and the boys to Madrid, Spain. Keith was assigned to the 1989th Communications Group at Torrejon Air Base.

During their three years in Spain, Keith worked in Job Control and Plans & Scheduling. He began writing as a hobby, and also built up a successful freelance photography business. He bowled well in tournaments during 1984, averaging about 190 and winning many second place finishes.

During his last year in Spain he also served as the Squadron Historian of the 2146th Communications Squadron. In this additional duty he was responsible for writing a quarterly history of the unit's operations and activities.

3

In January 1985 Keith, Joycelyn, and the boys left Spain. Since Keith had only a few months left on his enlistment, Joycelyn and the kids set up house in New Market, Alabama. Keith spent three months alone at the 5th Combat Communications Group at Robins AFB, Georgia, before out-processing the Air Force in early May.

On May 22, 1985 Jaron Michael was born at Huntsville Hospital. Unable to find an acceptable job, Keith returned to Robins AFB and reenlisted for four years on 2 July. The rest of the family joined him shortly after.

Shortly after reenlisting Keith requested retraining as a full-time Air Force historian. His request was approved in February 1986, and on 3 March he began his new job at the Warner Robins Air Logistics Center Office of History.

Becoming an Air Force historian renewed his interest in writing, and during the next year he had many articles and letters published in local newspapers and national magazines. He also began an intensive effort writing family history.

In August 1986 Keith began a world-wide effort to locate other graduates of overseas high schools. He was hoping to create a directory that these alumni could use to find old friends. Articles about him and his effort were published in more than a dozen newspapers around the world, however only a few hundred people replied. He abandoned this search in March 1987.

On February 3, 1987 Keith and Joycelyn's first daughter was born. Chelsea Nicole was born at Robins AFB Hospital at Warner Robins, Georgia.

In June 1987 Keith was reassigned to the Alaskan Air Command Office of History, headquartered at Elmendorf AFB. The family travelled more than 7,800 miles by car across the United States and Canada during their month-long trek to Anchorage, Alaska. During their trip they visited relatives in Alabama, Minnesota and Washington, old friends in Spokane, and saw Yellowstone Park.

Keith is presently the Assistant Command Historian of the Alaskan Air Command. In his job he is responsible for co-writing an annual history of the command, conducting oral histories and interviews, and writing special studies.

Keith serves as Deacon's Advisor in the Anchorage 1st Ward of the Church of Jesus Christ of Latter-day Saints, and is also Historian of the Anchorage Alaska North Stake.

(Current as of 16 April 1988)

APPENDIX G
Sample Oral History

Edward & Bessie Banks

an

Oral History

1955 – 1965

ORAL HISTORY INTERVIEW

of

EDWARD & BESSIE BANKS

10 May 1986

SUBJECT: Birth of first son, Keith

INTERVIEWER: Joycelyn G. Banks

Thirty years ago today Edward Banks and Bessie Grider were
married in Huntsville, Alabama. Their first son, Keith, was
born on 19 March 1957 in Spokane, Washington. This interview
took place in the Banks' family living room at 2805 Coosa
Circle, Huntsville, Alabama.

JOYCELYN: How did you feel when you first found out that you
were going to have a baby?

BESSIE: Back then, you got married and you had a baby. It was
just a fact of life. You weren't happy; you weren't sad. I
don't remember being real happy, and I definitely wasn't sad
about it - it was a fact of life. For me it was just something
that happened. [To Ed] What do you remember?

ED: I just remember it being a good thing, as long as it turned
out to be a boy (laughter in background).

BESSIE: That really worried me.

ED: A boy to get out and play ball with and do things like
that. I don't know what I would have done with a girl. She'd
just have been stuck in the kitchen doing dishes (more
laughter).

BESSIE: I don't remember feeling one way or the other. Babies were always there as far as I was concerned; there was one always coming or going when I was growing up. And I remember Ed already had Keith playing for the University of Minnesota. That's all he could talk about, and I would say "Ed, what if it's a girl?" He would say "It's not going to be a girl." He would not discuss a girl at all.

JOYCELYN: How did your pregnancy go? Were you really sick, or was there anything else you remember?

BESSIE: I craved snow, with soot in it (laughter). Ed would get real upset. I was seven months pregnant when we left Alabama going back to Washington. After we got to snow country I would make Ed stop along the side of the road and make me a snowball so I could eat it. I can remember so well him saying he wouldn't mind it so bad if he had Alabama tags on the car, but with those Washington plates on the car people were going to think he was crazy out there making snowballs.

We lived in that house on Cleveland, and before Ed would go to work in the morning he would go out and get me a snowball. We had a coal furnace, and soot would come out of it. I wanted it from where that soot came out on the snow.

JOYCELYN: Gave it more flavor?

BESSIE: I guess. But I had to have it every day. I had to have my fix.

ED: And I had to be careful there were no yellow streaks in it (laughter in background).

BESSIE: I just had a little morning sickness, and my snow, but that was all.

JOYCELYN: What kind of preparations did you make? Did you move into a bigger house?

BESSIE: No, we had a big enough house. It had two bedrooms in it. We bought a crib, and some play clothes.

JOYCELYN: When was the baby due?

BESSIE: He was due on Saint Patrick's Day.

JOYCELYN: So then he was two days late?

BESSIE: Yes.

JOYCELYN: How did you get to the hospital?

ED: Back about that time I used to have a little trouble with the car's gas gauge, and never did know exactly how low it would go before I would run out. I had run out two or three times before that. When we went to the hospital we were headed down the main street; it was just a four-lane road that went right down through Spokane and ended at the hospital. We were about half way to the hospital when the car sputtered and the motor quit. I looked at the gas gauge and it was down on empty, and I knew that I'd run out of gas. There wasn't much traffic, so I just cut across two lanes of traffic and coasted into a gas station and up to the first pump.

I remember getting out of the car and telling the man I needed some gas, and he asked me to pull up to the front pump (laughter in background). I told him I couldn't do that because I was out of gas. He wanted me to get up in front so somebody else could pull in behind me. I said "I can't go any further because I just ran out of gas." He went ahead and put some gas in and I paid him. We started up and I was able to get down to the hospital.

BESSIE: I wasn't really in labor. The doctor induced me.

JOYCELYN: Did you like your doctor? Was he good?

BESSIE: At the time I thought he was okay. I didn't like doctors, period. He was of the old school that didn't tell you anything: what he was doing; why he was doing it; or what was going to happen to you. He was going to do everything for you. I don't know if he was all that good or not.

JOYCELYN: Where was Ed when Keith was born?

BESSIE: In the waiting room, like all good fathers-to-be.

JOYCLEYN: Were you pacing the floor, or just nervous, or do you even remember?

ED: I don't think I was sitting there reading a book (laughter in background).

BESSIE: But I do remember one thing that I didn't like - [to Ed] Dr. Black told you that you had a boy. I didn't get to tell you. He told you, and I didn't think that was right. I thought I should be the one to tell. When he told me that it was a boy I said "Ed will be so happy." Then he went and told him.

JOYCELYN: Was Keith in his own room right from the start?

BESSIE: No, I think we put the crib in with us for a few weeks. He'd wake up and I didn't want to get up, so I'd get up and lay him on my stomach and we'd both go to sleep. The biggest adjustment for me to make after Keith was born was

3

washing those dirty diapers! It was awful. I came from a big family, but I never ever washed a dirty diaper. I can remember going into the bathroom and gagging. I was so sorry when Ed had to go back to work (laughter).

JOYCELYN: Was he changing diapers?

BESSIE: Yes. He started being a father right from the very beginning.

Change my diaper, Mom!

JOYCELYN: How did you divide things up, taking care of Keith? Who got up when he woke up during the night?

BESSIE: Whoever heard him. Ed was a helpful daddy from the beginning. He wasn't one of those fathers that slept on and didn't hear anything.

JOYCELYN: An eighties' father back in the fifties?

BESSIE: That's right; that's definitely right.

JOYCELYN: Do you remember how much money you were making when Keith was born?

ED: Not for sure, but I could come awful close. When Keith was born I was probably making around six and a half thousand dollars a year.

BESSIE: And we didn't have any health insurance.

JOYCELYN: So you paid all the bills?

BESSIE: Yeah. The way we worked that was every time I went to the doctor we paid him. And then the whole time that I was in the hospital when Keith was born Ed worked overtime just about every day. I think we paid that hospital bill with the overtime check.

ED: It was just a coincidence. We had a lot of trouble at work, and when she went in the hospital I went out and worked extra hours and made a bunch of overtime. When the bill came we just paid it off and it was almost as if nothing had happened.

BESSIE: But I think the total hospital bill was less than two hundred dollars.

Bessie, Keith, and Ed in front of home.

JOYCELYN: Did Keith get into a lot when he was a baby?

BESSIE: I remember him getting into the grease. I kept a Crisco can, and I'd poured the bacon grease and stuff in it and I kept it underneath the sink. He came into the living room one day - I was sitting in the living room - and he just jabbered and jabbered and jabbered (laughter in background). And I said "Okay, okay." He went crawling back into the kitchen and was real quiet. When I went in there, he was just sitting there, and he had poured that grease out and had it in his hair and in his face and just everywhere. I couldn't say a thing because I think I'd told him he could do it (more laughter). I think he came in and asked me and I said "Yeah, okay." And that stuff was a year old because I'd just been dumping it down in there. It was all over the floor, and all over him; I don't know how much of it he ate.

5

APPENDIX H
Sample Pedigree Chart

PEDIGREE CHART

CHART NO. 2-1

```
                                                                16 _____ CONT ON CHART  2-2
                                                    8  J. Thomas FOSTER
                                                       BORN              17 _____ CONT ON CHART  2-3
                                                       WHERE  NC
                                       4  William Pinkney FOSTER    WHEN MARRIED 31 Aug 1898
                                          BORN 31 Jul 1899          1904
                                          WHERE                     DIED
                                          WHEN MARRIED 10 Oct 1926  18  Benjamin Frank CAMPER
                                          DIED 5 Dec 1956        9  Susan F. CAMPER   CONT ON CHART  2-4
                                          WHERE.                    BORN 1869
                                                                    WHERE              19  Parnelia F. McCRARY  CONT ON CHART  2-5
                    2  William Don FOSTER                           DIED 1920
                       BORN 20 Aug 1927                             WHERE Madison Co., AL
                       WHERE Madison, AL                     10  Nicholas Donald CRUTCHER  20  James T. CRUTCHER  CONT ON CHART  2-6
                       WHEN MARRIED 16 Apr 1957                     BORN 23 Apr 1854
                       DIED                                         WHERE           AL
                       WHERE                                        WHEN MARRIED 3 Jan 1877  21  Margaret A.  CONT ON CHART  2-7
                                       5  Crucie Donnie CRUTCHER    DIED 4 Jan 1929
                                          BORN 11 Mar 1893          WHERE Madison Co., AL
                                          WHERE                  11  Crucie Elizor PIKE  22  William A. PIKE  CONT ON CHART  2-8
                                          DIED 17 Sep 1967          BORN May 1860
                                          WHERE                     WHERE        AL     23  Eliza Jane JOHNSON  CONT ON CHART  2-9
                                                                    DIED Jul 1901
                                                                    WHERE
 1  Jocyelyn Gay FOSTER                                       12  George Washington WILLCOX  24  Joseph WILCOX  CONT ON CHART  2-10
    BORN 5 Mar 1958                                                BORN 19 Dec 1878
    WHERE Huntsville, AL                                           WHERE              25 _____ CONT ON CHART  2-11
    WHEN MARRIED 16 Apr 1977          6  John Holden WILCOX        WHEN MARRIED 6 Jun 1900
    DIED                                 BORN 26 May 1909          DIED 23 Jan 1940
    WHERE                                WHERE Greenbriar, AL      WHERE Huntsville, AL  26  Eli TAYLOR  CONT ON CHART  2-12
    Keith Edward BANKS                   WHEN MARRIED 31 Jan 1926  13  Rowie Ann TAYLOR
    NAME OF HUSBAND OR WIFE              DIED 18 Mar 1985          BORN 15 Mar 1875
                                         WHERE Huntsville, AL      WHERE              27  Sarah Ann Elizabeth GAUTNEY  CONT ON CHART  2-13
                    3  Frances Elizabeth WILCOX                    DIED 11 May 1946
                       BORN 25 Mar 1931                            WHERE Huntsville, AL
                       WHERE Huntsville, AL                  14  John H. THOMAS  28  Rueben B. THOMAS  CONT ON CHART  2-14
                       DIED                                        BORN           1885
                       WHERE                                       WHERE
                                       7  Linnie Viola THOMAS      WHEN MARRIED 4 Feb 1906  29  Sarah  CONT ON CHART  2-15
                                          BORN 3 Sep 1909          DIED 9 Jun 1918
                                          WHERE Boma, TN          WHERE Nashville, TN
                                          DIED                  15  Sarah Frances WHITEHEAD  30  Felix P. WHITEHEAD  CONT ON CHART  2-16
                                          WHERE                    BORN 10 Nov 1887
                                                                   WHERE Boma, TN      31  Mary Jane FIELDS  CONT ON CHART  2-17
                                                                   DIED 7 Jan 1970
                                                                   WHERE San Francisco, CA
```

NO. 1 ON THIS CHART IS
THE SAME PERSON AS NO. _____
ON CHART NO.

SOURCES OF INFORMATION

PEDIGREE CHART

NO. 1 ON THIS CHART IS
THE SAME PERSON AS NO. _____
ON CHART NO. _____

Keith Edward BANKS
BORN 19 Mar 1957
WHERE Spokane, WA
WHEN MARRIED 16 Apr 1977
DIED
WHERE
Joycelyn Gay FOSTER
NAME OF HUSBAND OR WIFE

SOURCES OF INFORMATION

2 **Edward Waldo BANKS**
BORN 15 Feb 1933
WHERE Minneapolis, MN
WHEN MARRIED 10 May 1956
DIED
WHERE

3 **Bessie Fay GRIDER**
BORN 14 Sep 1936
WHERE Hollywood, AL
DIED
WHERE

4 **Charles Lemuel BANKS**
BORN 4 Sep 1893
WHERE Springfield, MD
WHEN MARRIED 10 Apr 1930
DIED 31 Dec 1973
WHERE Seattle, WA

5 **Ingrid Marie ERICKSON**
BORN 4 Jun 1905
WHERE Kent, MN
DIED
WHERE

6 **Aubry Dearly Van GRIDER**
BORN 28 Feb 1917
WHERE Hollywood, AL
WHEN MARRIED 4 Jul 1935
DIED 23 Dec 1978
WHERE Scottsboro, AL

7 **Jenisha Jane COOLEY**
BORN 19 May 1916
WHERE Hollywood, AL
DIED
WHERE

8 **Lemuel BANKS**
BORN 18 Dec 1859
WHERE Tod Township, PA
WHEN MARRIED 11 Apr 1889
DIED 20 Mar 1940
WHERE Proctorville, OH

9 **Eleanor LANE**
BORN 20 Sep 1864
WHERE IN
DIED 28 Dec 1902
WHERE Springfield, MD

10 **Michael ERICKSON**
BORN 8 Oct 1860
WHERE Runnhovda, Norway
WHEN MARRIED 29 Nov 1899
DIED 2 Feb 1950
WHERE Margie, MN

11 **Brita HAUSVIK**
BORN 19 Sep 1871
WHERE Haus, Norway
DIED 18 Mar 1951
WHERE Margie, MN

12 **Francis Marion GRIDER**
BORN 14 Feb 1857
WHERE Marion Co., KY
WHEN MARRIED 20 Aug 1894
DIED 1 Jan 1931
WHERE Jackson Co., AL

13 **Martha Louise GOLD**
BORN 1 Oct 1876/77
WHERE Jackson Co., TN
DIED 2 Nov 1953
WHERE Jackson Co., AL

14 **James William COOLEY**
BORN 20 Nov 1883
WHERE Marion Co., TN
WHEN MARRIED
DIED 2 Apr 1949
WHERE Belifonte, AL

15 **Lucinda Annie Jane SMITH**
BORN 16 Nov 1886
WHERE
DIED 22 Mar 1972
WHERE Scottsboro, AL

16 **Joseph BANKS**
CONT. ON CHART 1-2

17 **Deborah EVERETT**
CONT. ON CHART 1-3

18 **Henry S. LANE**
CONT. ON CHART 1-4

19 **Rebecca Jane RYKER**
CONT. ON CHART 1-5

20 **Johannes Erickson RUNNHOVDA**
CONT. ON CHART 1-6

21 **Kari Mikjelsdotter VAKSDAL**
CONT. ON CHART 1-7

22 **Anders Mikjelson BOGO**
CONT. ON CHART 1-8

23 **Agdta Einarsdotter HAUSVIK**
CONT. ON CHART 1-9

24 **Joseph GUIDER**
CONT. ON CHART 1-10

25 **TUCK**
CONT. ON CHART 1-11

26 **Elijah D. GOLD**
CONT. ON CHART 1-12

27 **Frances WININGER**
CONT. ON CHART 1-13

28 **Jessie COOLEY**
CONT. ON CHART 1-14

29 CONT. ON CHART 1-15

30 **Isaac SMITH**
CONT. ON CHART 1-16

31 **Mary Jane HICKS**
CONT. ON CHART 1-17

APPENDIX I
Sample Family Group Sheet

HUSBAND Keith Edward BANKS

Born 19 Mar 1957 Place Spokane, Spokane, WA

Chr. Place

Marr. 16 Apr 1977 Place Huntsville, Madison, AL

Died Place

Bur. Place

HUSBAND'S FATHER Edward Waldo BANKS

HUSBAND'S MOTHER Bessie Fay GRIDER

HUSBAND'S OTHER WIVES

WIFE Joycelyn Gay FOSTER

Born 5 Mar 1958 Place Huntsville, Madison, AL

Chr. Place

Died Place

Bur. Place

WIFE'S FATHER William Don FOSTER

WIFE'S MOTHER Frances Elizabeth WILCOX

WIFE'S OTHER HUSBANDS

SEX M/F	CHILDREN Last each child (whether living or dead) in order of birth Given Names Surname	WHEN BORN DAY	MONTH	YEAR	WHERE BORN TOWN	COUNTY	STATE OR COUNTRY	DATE OF FIRST MARRIAGE TO WHOM	WHEN DIED DAY	MONTH	YEAR
1 M	Nathan Edward BANKS	14	Aug	1979	Wichita Falls	Wichita	TX				
2 M	Ryan David BANKS	2	May	1981	Athens	Limestone	AL				
3 M	Jaron Michael BANKS	22	May	1985	Huntsville	Madison	AL				
4 F	Chelsea Nicole BANKS	3	Feb	1987	Warner Robins	Houston	GA				
5											
6											
7											
8											
9											
10											
11											

SOURCES OF INFORMATION

OTHER MARRIAGES

HUSBAND Aubrey Pearly Von GRIDER

Born 28 Feb 1917   Place Hollywood, Jackson, AL
Chr.   Place
Marr. 4 Jul 1935   Place Hollywood, Jackson, AL
Died 23 Dec 1978   Place Scottsboro, Jackson, AL
Bur. 25 Dec 1978   Place Hollywood, Jackson, AL
HUSBAND'S FATHER Francis Marion GRIDER
HUSBAND'S MOTHER Martha Louisa GOLD
HUSBAND'S OTHER WIVES

WIFE Jerusha Jane COOLEY

Born 19 May 1916   Place Hollywood, Jackson, AL
Chr.   Place
Died   Place
Bur.   Place
WIFE'S FATHER James William COOLEY
WIFE'S MOTHER Lucinda Annie Jane SMITH
WIFE'S OTHER HUSBANDS

SEX M/F	CHILDREN — List each child (whether living or dead) in order of birth — Given Names	Surname	WHEN BORN DAY	MONTH	YEAR	WHERE BORN TOWN	COUNTY	STATE OR COUNTRY	DATE OF FIRST MARRIAGE TO WHOM	DAY	WHEN DIED MONTH	YEAR
1 X F	Bessie Fay	GRIDER	14	Sep	1936	Hollywood	Jackson	AL	10 May 1956 Edward Waldo BANKS			
2 F	Billie Iris	GRIDER	29	Dec	1938	Hollywood	Jackson	AL	1 Nov 1957 Victor CALDONNA			
3 F	Mazie Marie	GRIDER	12	Jan	1941	Hollywood	Jackson	AL		21	Nov	1958
4 M	Perry Rayford	GRIDER	17	Dec	1942	Hollywood	Jackson	AL	Patricia CAVES	18	May	1987
5 F	Orna Gayle	GRIDER	11	May	1945	Hollywood	Jackson	AL	24 Aug 1965 Donald MALISKEY, Jr.			
6 M	Aubrey Hurley	GRIDER	22	Mar	1947	Hollywood	Jackson	AL	20 Mar 1971 Jane BAKER			
7 F	Regina Jane	GRIDER	6	May	1949	Hollywood	Jackson	AL	3 Jun 1967 George Albert PIPES			
8 F	Darlene Angela	GRIDER	7	Oct	1951	Toft	Lincoln	TN	27 Jun 1970 Donald Ray SWING			
9 M	James Michael	GRIDER	13	Sep	1952	Toft	Lincoln	TN	Glenda Manning 8 Sep 1973			
10 F	Rita Joyce	GRIDER	18	Aug	1955	Ardmore	Giles	TN	Bobby Ray DOOSLEY			
11 F	Vicky Gay	GRIDER	17	Oct	1957	Scottsboro	Jackson	AL	Ronnie WRIGHT			

SOURCES OF INFORMATION

OTHER MARRIAGES
② V.E. JOHNSON

BIBLIOGRAPHY

Writing & Editing

CHICAGO MANUAL OF STYLE. University of Chicago Press, 1982. Style guide, including printing, typesetting, and grammar.

THE ELEMENTS OF STYLE, by William Strunk, Jr., and E. B. White. Coast to Coast Books, 1983. Fundamentals of writing, grammar, and style.

HARBRACE COLLEGE HANDBOOK, by John Hodges and Mary Whitten. Harcourt Brace Jovanovich, 1982. Reference guide to grammar and style.

YOUR LIFE STORY, by Earlynne Webber. Echo Publishing Company, 1984. How to write and publish the story of your life.

CHANGING MEMORIES INTO MEMOIRS, by Fanny-Maude Evans. Barnes & Noble, 1984. A good book for learning how to make your family history writing better and more interesting.

PRESERVING YOUR PAST, by Janice T. Dixon and Dora D. Flack. Doubleday, 1977. Excellent book on researching, organizing, and writing your personal history.

WRITE THE STORY OF YOUR LIFE, by Ruth Kanin. Elsevier-Dutton Publishing, 1981. Alex Haley says this is the "finest book on the subject."

HOW TO WRITE THE STORY OF YOUR LIFE, by Frank P. Thomas. Writer's Digest Books, 1984. Excellent how-to guide for writing an autobiography.

LIFE WRITING: A GUIDE TO FAMILY JOURNALS AND PERSONAL MEMOIRS, by William J. Hofmann. St. Martin's Press, 1982. A practical guide to writing and preserving life's experiences.

HOW TO WRITE AND SELL YOUR PERSONAL EXPERIENCES, by Lois Duncan. Writer's Digest Books, 1982. Excellent guide to writing about your personal experiences, whether for publication or just your own family.

WRITING FOR THE JOY OF IT, by Leonard L. Knott. Writer's Digest Books, 1983. Includes chapters on writing letters, diaries, autobiographies, family histories, cookbooks, plays, and children's stories.

THE NEW DIARY, by Tristine Rainer. J.P. Tarcher, 1978. Covers many of the uses and methods of journal writing.

KEEPING YOUR PERSONAL JOURNAL, by George F. Simons. Paulist Press, 1978. Includes discussion of the reasons people keep journals, and some different applications.

INSTANT ORAL BIOGRAPHIES, by William Zimmerman. Guarionex Press, 1981. As the title implies, a good how-to book for creating oral histories.

RECORDING YOUR FAMILY HISTORY, by William Fletcher. Dodd, Meade, & Company, 1986. One of the best sources for ideas, topics, and questions to use when preparing for an oral history interview.

VIDEO FAMILY PORTRAITS, by Rob Huberman and Laura Janis. Heritage Books, 1987. An excellent guide for anyone interested in conducting an oral history, and a must for the person filming the interview.

ORAL HISTORY FROM TAPE TO TYPE, by Cullom Davis. American Library Association, 1977. One of the best guides to transcribing oral history interviews.

PUBLISHING NEWSLETTERS, by Howard Penn Hudson. Charles Scribner's Sons, 1982. An excellent guide to style and design of newsletters; includes many samples.

EDITING YOUR NEWSLETTER, by Mark Beach. Coast to Coast Books, 1988. From content to design to reproduction, one of the best guides to designing and publishing a newsletter.

GENEALOGICAL RESEARCH ESSENTIALS, by Norman E. Wright and David H. Pratt. Bookcraft, 1967. One of the best and most comprehensive books on the elements of genealogical research.

THE TIMETABLES OF AMERICAN HISTORY, Laurence Urdang, Editor. Simon & Schuster, 1983. Presents major political, arts, sciences, and miscellaneous events in America and elsewhere in easy to read tables from the year 1000 to 1980.

THE TIMETABLES OF HISTORY, by Bernard Grun. Simon & Schuster, 1979. Comprehensive chronological tables of historical events from politics, literature, theater, religion, philosophy, visual arts, music, science, and daily life from 5000 BC to 1978 AD.

THE MAP CATALOG, Joel Makower, Editor. Tilden Press, 1986. An excellent reference book to help the family historian find maps of relevance to their family's history.

THE HERALDRY BOOK: A GUIDE TO DESIGNING YOUR OWN COAT OF ARMS, by Marvin Grosswirth. Doubleday, 1981. As the title indicates, an excellent guide for designing a coat of arms from scratch.

AN HERALDIC ALPHABET, by J.P. Brooke-Little. Arco Publishing, 1973. A comprehensive glossary of heraldic terminology with over 300 drawings.

Self-Publishing, Printing, & Bookbinding

THE COMPLETE GUIDE TO SEIF-PUBLISHING, by Tom & Marilyn Ross. Writer's Digest Books, 1985. An excellent and comprehensive guide covering the many facets of book production and marketing.

THE SELF-PUBLISHING MANUAL, by Dan Poynter. Para Publications, 1984. Covers the many aspects of creating your own books.

GETTING IT PRINTED, by Mark Beach, Steve Shepro, Ken Russon. Coast to Coast Books, 1986. Whether you're creating a newsletter, pamphlet, or book, this book explains everything you'll need to know about getting it printed.

BOOKMAKING: THE ILLUSTRATED GUIDE TO DESIGN, PRODUCTION, AND EDITING, by Marshall Lee. R.R. Bowker, 1979. One of the standard works in the field of bookmaking.

BOOKBINDING. Boy Scouts of America Merit Badge Series, 1969. Contains simple, illustrated guide to hardcover binding of books.

SIMPLIFIED BOOKBINDING, by Henry Gross. Charles Scribner's Sons, 1976. A very good, illustrated guide to binding your own books.

BOOKBINDING, by Arthur W. Johnson. Thames and Hudson, 1978. Definitely the best book I've seen on the subject, with more than 250 illustrations.

FINE BOOKBINDING IN THE TWENTIETH CENTURY, by Roy Harley Lewis. Arco Publishing, 1985. Not a how-to book, but an excellent idea book to quality bookbinding, with scores of photographs showing the original work and designs that others have created.

ABOUT THE AUTHOR

Keith Banks was born March 19, 1957 in Spokane, Washington. In the years since, he has lived in Cherry Hill, New Jersey; El Paso, Texas; Mundelein, Illinois; Pirmasens, West Germany; Huntsville, Alabama; Seoul, South Korea; Taipei, Taiwan; Wichita Falls, Texas; Austin, Texas; Osan Air Base, South Korea; Madrid, Spain; Warner Robins, Georgia; and Anchorage, Alaska. He is an Air Force historian (by occupation), a church historian (by calling), and a family historian (by love). Keith is married to the former Joycelyn Foster of Huntsville, Alabama, and they have four children: Nathan, Ryan, Jaron, and Chelsea.

ABOUT THE ILLUSTRATOR

Jim Parrish is an award-winning illustrator living in Anchorage, Alaska. He has been an Air Force graphic artist for eighteen years, and has been illustrating professionally for more than a quarter century. He has done considerable freelance commercial work, including fine art for advertising agencies. The Georgia-born artist lived in Michigan and Texas during his youth, and since joining the Air Force has lived in Texas, Florida, Okinawa, Japan, Arkansas, and Korea.

You're Invited . . .

The author encourages comments and suggestions about the content of this book. Thousands of people are already successfully documenting their personal and family histories, some in ways not discussed in this book. If you feel you have an idea that might help others preserve their own family heritage, please write the author in care of the publisher. Your comments and suggestions may be incorporated into future editions of this work.

INDEX